Differentiated Instruction

GROUPING FOR SUCCESS

Vicki Gibson, Ph.D.
Jan Hasbrouck, Ph.D.

Boston   Burr Ridge, IL   Dubuque, IA   Madison, WI   New York
San Francisco   St. Louis   Bangkok   Bogotá   Caracas   Kuala Lumpur
Lisbon   London   Madrid   Mexico City   Milan   Montreal   New Delhi
Santiago   Seoul   Singapore   Sydney   Taipei   Toronto

Higher Education

McGraw-Hill Higher Education
A Division of The McGraw-Hill Companies

3 4 5 6 7 8 9 0 QPD/QPD 0 9 8 7

ISBN: 978-0-07-337849-7
MHID: 0-07-337849-6

Editor in Chief: *Emily Barrosse*
Publisher: *Beth Mejia*
Sponsoring Editor: *Allison McNamara*
Marketing Manager: *Sarah Martin*
Editorial Coordinator: *Emily Pecora*
Production Editor: *Karol Jurado*
Production Service: *Matrix Productions Inc.*
Manuscript Editor: *Ann Whetstone*
Design Coordinator: *Margarite Reynolds*
Art Editor: *Emma Ghiselli*
Illustrator: *Nugraphic Design, Inc.*
Photo Research: *Nora Agbayani*
Production Supervisor: *Richard DeVitto*
Composition: *9.5/13 Stone Serif by Noyes Composition and Graphics*
Printing: *45# New Era Matte Plus, Quebecor World/Dubuque, IA*

Library of Congress Cataloging-in-Publication Data
Gibson, Vicki.
  Differentiated instruction : grouping for success / Vicki Gibson, Jan Hasbrouck. — 1st ed.
     p. cm.
  Includes bibliographical references.
  ISBN-13: 978-0-07-337849-7
  ISBN-10: 0-07-337849-6
 1. Individualized instruction. 2. Mixed ability grouping in education. 3. Elementary school teaching. I. Hasbrouck, Jan E. (Jan Elizabeth) II. Title.
LB1031.G535 2008
371.2'52—dc22

                                       2007010568

www.mhhe.com

Differentiated Instruction

GROUPING FOR SUCCESS

CONTENTS

ABOUT THE AUTHORS

For more than a decade, Dr. Gibson and Dr. Hasbrouck have collaborated on a number of projects. They share a passion for and a commitment to helping schools reach the goal of helping every student become a reader.

VICKI GIBSON, Ph.D. With professional experience at the primary level in public and private education, as well as in higher education, Vicki Gibson has a solid understanding of theoretical models and current research. However, *Differentiated Instruction: Grouping for Success* is not based on theory alone.

Dr. Gibson writes from the vantage point of more than 30 years of firsthand experience in a variety of classrooms. She developed the suggestions presented in this book while teaching for 10 years in public schools, then implemented them in her own primary schools and also while teaching at Texas A&M University. The basic framework has been successfully replicated in numerous classrooms, providing skills-focused, differentiated instruction for early childhood, elementary and secondary students. The author's own curriculum, developed for her schools and published as the *We Can! Early Childhood Curriculum*, embraces the tenets and techniques outlined in this guide. Dr. Gibson works as a national consultant, teacher trainer, and author. She is the President of Longmire Learning Center, Inc., in College Station, Texas.

JAN HASBROUCK, Ph.D. Jan Hasbrouck has worked as an educator for over 30 years, first as a reading specialist and later as a university professor and researcher. She is now the president of a consulting company that advises state agencies, school districts, and schools in the United States and internationally about best practices in reading instruction. Her interests include the role that reading coaches can play in supporting students and teachers. She is the co-author of a handbook for coaches and administrators: *The Reading Coach: A How-to Manual for Success.*

FOREWORD

There simply could not be a better team than Vicki Gibson and Jan Hasbrouck to address the research and practice implications for differentiating instruction with a special emphasis on varying instructional groups to meet students' needs.

Perhaps one of the most challenging aspects of teaching is determining how to organize instruction so that all students learn, rather than just teaching to the middle and hoping for the best. Consider this, typical teachers have in their classrooms a range of students from those with disabilities to those who are academically gifted. How can one teacher reasonably meet the needs of this range of learners? This book is an excellent resource for clear and practical ideas about how to approach this challenge.

There are many theoretical frameworks for differentiating instruction, but this book provides more than theory. With professional experiences at the primary level in public and private education, as well as in higher education, Vicki Gibson and Jan Hasbrouck have a deep knowledge of how research and practice come together to invigorate instruction.

I think you will enjoy learning about how to differentiate instruction through assessment and data management and then how to use their data management system to group for instruction. These authors also provide very useful ideas about how to organize classrooms and schedules and how to use rotation charts to help students work efficiently in various grouping structures. They also teach practical and sensible ways to coach for success so that this book can be used not just by practicing teachers but also by coaches and school district leaders.

Meeting the diverse needs of students is an ongoing challenge for teachers and educational leaders. This book provides the sound theoretical, research, and practical suggestions needed to assist educators in making a difference in the lives of the students they teach.

SHARON VAUGHN, Ph.D.

INTRODUCTION

Imagine a classroom of 28 students. Six students learn new vocabulary and read with the teacher at one table. Eight students sort vocabulary words at the work-table, helping one another collaboratively. Eight more students work at various learning centers called "workstations," some work collaboratively, others may work independently. Meanwhile, 6 more students read leveled, self-selected books at their desks, independently or with a partner.

When two students begin to talk loudly at the workstation, the Voice Level Monitor quietly signals to them to lower their voices. After 15 minutes, the Time Keeper quietly warns each group that it is almost time to move to a different activity, saying, "Five minutes until we change." At this time, the students begin to wrap up their work and the teacher begins to bring the lesson to closure. When a timer goes off, some students read individually or with a partner. Others complete assigned jobs, checking workstations.

The whole group reconvenes either at their desks or a designated place. The teacher then conducts a 10–15 minute whole class lesson. Then a student serving as the Chart Caller reads aloud student names on the rotation chart and helps direct them to the correct places or facilitates in their choice of a workstation. Students serving as Workstation Monitors quietly and quickly ensure that each workstation is tidy and adequately supplied for a new group. A Worktable Monitor ensures the same for the worktable. After a 2 minute transition, each student is engaged in the correct activity in the correct place: workstation, worktable, desk, or teaching table. When two students begin to squabble at the worktable, a student serving as a Counselor intervenes to ensure a peaceable and speedy solution while the teacher continues to teach with focus and serenity at the teaching table.

This scenario sounds too good to be true, right? Perhaps it sounds like something out of *Ideals* or *Pollyanna*. Yet it need not be an impossible dream or beyond reach. With the right tools and with careful coaching, this scenario could be realized in many classrooms, regardless of students' ages, student grade levels, or the academic content.

There is convincing evidence that educators in America are working extremely hard to manage classrooms and instruction. Most teachers expend tremendous energy planning lessons, managing student behaviors, meeting demands for assessment, and individualizing curricula to help students achieve district, state, and national standards. Some are more successful than others, but the unique challenge for most teachers who want to differentiate instruction involves managing whole class and small group instruction. Teachers need routines or procedures for implementing differentiated instruction successfully in their classrooms. This book meets that need.

Differentiating instruction in response to student variance is a hot topic in educational conversations. Continuing failure rates amongst student populations produce convincing arguments that traditional whole class lecture formats have proven ineffective for individualizing instruction and providing the learning support some students need (USDOE, 2002). Despite the fact that differentiating instruction to attend to student variance makes sense conceptually, challenges for implementation exist because there is no agreement on procedural models that demonstrate how to make it happen successfully in classrooms.

Successful models for implementation and replication are in short supply. They must be created, applied in the field, and researched to validate their effectiveness before becoming a standard for classroom practice. Teachers need professional development that helps them understand what differentiated instruction is and how it can be implemented before they are held accountable for making it happen successfully in their classrooms.

Despite the paucity of researched models for differentiating instruction, some components, particularly grouping for instruction, have been validated and proven effective for increasing reading achievement with students failing to make grade-level requirements (Elbaum, Vaughn, Hughes, & Moody, 1998; Elbaum, Vaughn, Hughes, Moody, & Schumm, 2000a). According to grouping research, increasing small group differentiated instruction leads to an increase in reading achievement (Lou, Abrami, Spence, Poulsen, Chambers, & d'Appolonia, 1996; Mathes & Fuchs, 1994; Moody, Vaughn, & Schumn, 1997).

In order to address the widening range of instruction within one classroom, teachers must use data-informed, small group instruction with an instructional purpose specifically designed to meet students' needs (Kosanovich, Ladinsky, Nelson, & Torgesen, 2006). There is general agreement that differentiated instruction is an alternative approach for teaching that attends to individual variances and needs (Fountas & Pinnell, 1996; Tileston, 2000; Tomlinson, 2000; Tomlinson & Eidson, 2003). This book provides a teacher-friendly link from research to practice and discusses the methodology for implementing differentiated instruction successfully in classrooms.

The purpose of this book is to provide field-tested, research-based routines and procedures that help teachers organize classrooms and differentiate instruction consistently to positively affect student achievement. Teaching tools are included to help teachers group students for instruction, manage whole class and small group instruction, and incorporate flexible grouping practices and repeated practice opportunities that enhance student achievement. Each chapter's content has been designed so educators may apply the tools immediately in their practice. Each chapter ends with a list of resources that extend learning opportunities or support instruction.

Chapter 1 provides an overview of the research and literature for best practices for differentiating instruction. Chapter 2 suggests ways for teachers to integrate assessment with instruction and become data-informed about students' needs and progress. Chapter 3 discusses how to group students for instruction in response to student variance in classrooms. Chapters 4 and 5 provide teaching tools that create routines and procedures to manage whole class and small group instruction so as to use teaching time efficiently and effectively. Chapter 6 provides suggestions for coaching to improve instructional effectiveness so that teachers, coaches, and administrators work together to achieve positive change and outcomes. The appendices include forms or checklists to ensure high fidelity of implementation of a management system for whole class and small group instruction that includes explicit instruction, guided practice opportunities, progress monitoring, and program evaluation.

This book helps teachers and administrators use a management system that includes flexible grouping practices that successfully differentiate instruction and address increasing student variance in classrooms. The text explains how to develop and use a management system to implement whole class and small group differentiated instruction. After reading this book, teachers will have an answer to their most frequently asked questions: (1) How am I supposed to get everything done and teach small groups? (2) What are the rest of the students doing when I am teaching a small group?

ACKNOWLEDGMENTS

I want to express my heartfelt gratitude to family and friends who provided encouragement during my life as a learner, teacher, mom, and Mimi. Thank you for constantly blessing me with your love, presence, and wisdom.

I am grateful for numerous adventures and projects that I have shared with Jan Hasbrouck. Her friendship, heart, and soul have provided guidance, wisdom, and stability many times in my life. What an incredible journey we have had!

—Vicki Gibson, Ph.D.

I am honored to have had this opportunity to collaborate with my esteemed colleague and dear friend, Dr. Vicki Gibson, and to share the wonderful ideas for classroom organization that she has been developing and perfecting for so many years. I dedicate my work on this project to the teachers, coaches, and principals who work so hard—everyday—to provide the best instruction possible to *every* student.

—Jan Hasbrouck, Ph.D.

Jan and I were honored by many highly respected experts who reviewed this manuscript and provided great guidance. We are eternally grateful to:

Nader Darehshori, former CEO, Houghton Mifflin, whose commitment to education and helping others has inspired many of us to seek excellence. We are thankful for his review of our manuscript and advice.

Susan Ebbers, M.S., whose edits to the initial manuscripts held us accountable for finally putting our practice into words. Thanks to a wise colleague and friend!

Joe Torgesen, Ph.D., whose research, instruction, and leadership have improved teaching and learning at all levels. You are a major influence on our work!

Sharon Vaughn, Ph.D., whose brilliant research, professional leadership, and personal friendship encouraged us to link research to practice through this work. Thanks for being a catalyst for educational reform and improvement!

Zoe Ann Brown, Ph.D., Laurie Mounce, Marsha Sonnenberg, Deb Steinbacher, Vickie Whitfield, and the staff at Longmire Learning Center, whose insights from classroom teachers' eyes kept us grounded in practical application and reality.

We owe many thanks to the great folks from Macmillan McGraw-Hill and Matrix Productions for your contributions, kindness, and patience.

Thanks for the encouragement and leadership from Valery Levy, Daniela Perelli, and Susan Rivers. We are energized by your passion and dedication to improving teaching and learning! We, as many others, are blessed by your work.

—From both authors

CHAPTER 1

Differentiating Instruction

IDENTIFYING WHAT THE LITERATURE AND RESEARCH REPORT ABOUT differentiating instruction and clarifying what it is and what it is not is critical to understanding the topic. Numerous publications are available that describe the characteristics of differentiated instruction or suggest activities that can be modified to address student variance. Those materials are an important support for teachers and administrators who need to get a visual for how differentiating instruction can look in a classroom. Understanding the concept is crucial for high fidelity of implementation and for assessing outcomes or measuring changes in practice. However, teachers also need research-based methodology for teaching differently or for establishing the routines and procedures that create opportunities for differentiated instruction to occur.

Developing classrooms that positively affect student achievement by providing differentiated instruction tailored to students' specific needs is a common trait of highly successful schools. What is not so common is teacher training that demonstrates how to use routines and procedures for managing whole and small group lessons and incorporating differentiated instruction. This chapter clarifies what differentiated instruction is, and the remainder of the book describes tools for successful implementation.

Differentiated instruction or teaching differently is necessary to address the diversity of students' needs. Traditional practice using whole group lecture format is not working. The increase in student variance in classrooms, often described as a disparity in skills and knowledge, has become a huge challenge for teachers who are responsible for providing high-quality instruction to enhance student achievement. Teachers are asked to use data to determine students' needs, select curricula, and group students for instruction. They are expected to teach, monitor progress, and reteach as needed. Teachers are told to teach in small groups and differentiate instruction to address specific student needs.

Most teachers report they have received minimal training or professional development that prepares them for such tasks. Improving instruction through professional development means providing teachers with the knowledge and skills they need to provide differentiated instruction by teaching students in smaller groups. Interestingly, many teachers report that teaching in small groups is not the problem. Managing whole class and small group instruction and getting everything done is the problem. The lack of procedural models for implementing differentiated instruction must be addressed.

Scientific research has not provided procedural models for differentiating instruction partially because of the ambiguity surrounding what it is and the limited research on how to implement it successfully in classrooms. The lack of a clear focus or a procedural model complicates issues for research and replication. In an effort to clarify expectations, the Florida Center for Reading Research (FCRR, 2006) presented this definition of differentiated instruction: "matching instruction to meet the different needs of learners in a given classroom that includes small groups and increased practice opportunities in the form of reading centers." While the definition describes the concept, it does not provide the methodology for making it happen in classrooms. More research is needed to develop a conceptual understanding of differentiated instruction and its application in classrooms.

Scientific research has identified components associated with differentiated instruction, that is, the critical elements necessary for matching instruction to the different needs of learners for reading instruction. But a research-to-practice gap exists in education that inhibits change (Foorman & Torgesen, 2001; Hart & Risley, 1995; National Reading Panel, 2000). There is compelling evidence regarding what works to provide explicit skills-based reading instruction, but educators are not taking advantage of research-based practices in classrooms (Gersten, Vaughn, Deshler, & Schiller, 1997; Lyon, 1995; National Institute for Literacy, 2002; National Reading Panel, 2000). Unfortunately, teachers report they have no time to read research, nor do they receive professional development in best practices for improving instructional delivery. Understanding conceptually what differentiated instruction is and what it is not will be critical to successful implementation in classrooms.

UNDERSTANDING THE CONCEPT OF DIFFERENTIATED INSTRUCTION

A general consensus needs to be established about a definition of differentiated instruction and the kind of professional development needed to improve instruction using whole class and small group lessons. Current literature includes multiple descriptive characteristics regarding what differentiation looks like in classrooms. Many materials are available that discuss the need to improve content, curriculum, and delivery and to define ways to assess students' needs (FCRR, 2006; Hart & Risley, 1995; Tomlinson & Edison, 2003). Other literature explains how to modify lessons and activities to differentiate instruction (Fountas & Pinnell, 1996; Tyner & Green, 2004). Regardless, instructional delivery, or how teachers teach, has been slow to change.

Teachers often rely on personal educational experiences as their model for good instruction. They teach the way they learned. Traditional whole class lecture formats prevail because they are a familiar habit and environment. Reading instruction provided in traditional whole class lecture format has been criticized because it restricts opportunities for individualizing instruction. Teaching to the mass fails to address the needs of all learners (Vaughn et al., 1998). Student-responsive, multitiered small group instruction is supported because it improves reading achievement (Hall, 2002; Tilly, 2003; Vaughn, 2003).

However, there is no empirical evidence that validates the effectiveness of differentiated instruction (Tilly, 2003). Ambiguity in the definition and lack of a procedural model has made it difficult to define, implement, or conduct research. Grouping for instruction, a hallmark characteristic of differentiated instruction, has been researched and proven effective, and while that is a significant contribution to the knowledge base for improving instruction, it is only one piece of the puzzle for differentiation.

Simply teaching students in smaller groups is not necessarily differentiating instruction. Grouping is a procedural change for how we teach. In order to differentiate, changes in what we teach are also needed. That means data-informed teaching using leveled materials that match text difficulty to student reading levels and leading skills-focused lessons that include more student engagement, and guided practice with constructive feedback from a teacher or a peer. Grouping creates opportunities for teachers to teach differently, but changes must also occur in the instructional content and types of lesson structures or activities used in small groups. Classroom reading instruction in small groups is not differentiated when all students receive the same instruction or use the same lessons and materials. Using the same content in a different presentation, that is, teaching in smaller groups, is only minimally responsive to diverse needs. Responding to student variance requires that two things change: what is taught and how it is presented. Using smaller groups for instruction and alternating time periods for whole class and small groups creates an environment where teachers can deliver differentiated, responsive teaching.

The research on grouping for instruction reports positive changes in student outcomes. Research findings reveal that students receiving instruction in small groups learned significantly more than students who were not instructed in small groups (Lou et al., 1996; Mathes & Fuchs, 1994; Moody et al., 1997). This occurred when instruction and materials used in the small groups were adjusted for specific student needs. Data helps teachers provide explicit skills-focused instruction that is academically profitable for each student in a small group. The smaller group size increases opportunities for students to respond or stay engaged. Teachers hear and see students' responses and can provide immediate constructive feedback. In simple terms, the goal is to provide small group differentiated instruction by a highly skilled teacher to increase student achievement. In order to realize this goal, some old attitudes regarding what constitute a right and proper learning environment may need to be reviewed. For many, this can require updating our thinking about effective teaching and learning, as described below.

CONCEPTUALIZING A NEW MIND-SET
ABOUT DIFFERENTIATION

This new conceptualization involves a change in attitude and practice at all levels. Educators must embrace collaborative learning in classroom environments where students are encouraged to work in small groups and follow the modeling of a teacher or peer. In other words, they are encouraged and allowed to share work with others when learning a new skill. Teachers have to dispel the old notion that copying is cheating. Copying a model is viewed as an efficient and effective learning experience. During initial instruction, students work together to read text and complete activities so they can verbalize information, ask questions, and create deeper understandings.

Students' work is shared during initial practice activities and may be completed with a partner or in a small group. Shared learning experiences help students use curriculum materials and participate in activities in ways that deepen comprehension and enhance success. Allowing students to work in small collaborative groups is viewed positively because instruction continues as students assist each other by providing feedback. Collaborative learning allows students to seek help from a peer when the teacher is unavailable. It allows teachers to spend more time teaching rather than managing behaviors or responding to questions and facilitating learning in the classroom environment. The teacher focuses on instruction, while students work in groups or independently at a desk after sufficient instruction and guided practice have occurred.

Implementing differentiated instruction requires teachers to form small, student groupings where each student receives instruction that is academically profitable for specific needs. The grouping mind-set is supportive and not competitive, inclusive and not exclusive. Teachers must consider four factors important for implementing small group instruction.

1. *Group size*   How many students will work successfully in a small group to complete a specific lesson (e.g., smaller group sizes for students needing more intervention and explicit instruction, such as 3–5 students per group for struggling readers, or larger groups for practice activities or for students working on grade level with similar skill sets)

2. *Frequency*   How often each group meets with the teacher (e.g., preferably daily, if schedules permit, or at least two to three small group time periods per week)

3. *Duration*   How much time each group will spend with the teacher (e.g., 15–20 minutes, realizing that skill levels and amount of instruction needed will vary due to the length of time required for students to complete specific activities)

4. *Type of lesson structure*   Lesson purpose influences decision making about grouping whether it is for instructional, guided practice, or independent practice. The lesson purpose is important because newly introduced skills or concepts require more teacher support whereas guided practice lessons using previously learned skills are student directed. For many practice sessions, students can serve as peer tutors and the teacher's role is to guide and monitor instruction while determining needs or next steps to reteach, provide more guided practice, or advance to next objective.

TEACHING, THEN FACILITATING PRACTICE

Students benefit from more teaching. Teachers must manage instructional time efficiently to increase teaching and improve student outcomes. Often there is some confusion about the difference between explicit teaching and facilitated practice. Teaching involves preparing mentally and thinking about how to effectively deliver the instruction. When teachers explicitly teach, they visually and verbally model to demonstrate and clarify expectations and concepts. They explain and make information meaningful to the learner. Teachers observe students' responses while they teach and provide positive constructive feedback to support successful learning. They read text to and with students and discuss its meaning. Teaching occurs when teachers actively engage with students by leading the lesson and student learning.

Students listen to and participate in teacher-led explicit instruction. They interact with other peers and ask questions under the close supervision and guidance of a skillful teacher. Teachers guide the practice, analyze error patterns, and use data to inform and adjust instruction as needed. Students are taught when they are actively and personally engaged with a peer or teacher who can provide support and feedback to enhance comprehension and performance.

Conversely, facilitated practice is not teacher-led, explicit instruction. It is practice that is facilitated or supported using workbook pages, games, special projects, or technology. Teachers may monitor facilitated practice and consider that a guided practice activity, but when the teacher is unavailable for providing constructive feedback, the activity is unguided facilitated practice, not teaching. There is no teacher-led instruction because no support is there for the learner to get help. Teachers facilitate practice when they

- assign written work or special projects for students to complete at areas other than the teaching table, or have students complete workbook pages, write responses to problems or questions in a textbook, or write sentences with newly introduced vocabulary words.

- observe students conducting experiments or completing special projects as they work with peers who lack the skills for providing constructive feedback and assisting others.

- monitor performance by walking around the classroom and checking student folders or contracts to monitor progress, check completion of assignments, or grade papers after an activity has occurred.

Some lessons that are intended to be teaching opportunities can become a test. Either students can or cannot perform the tasks successfully depending on their former instruction. When students are expected to complete an activity independently before sufficient instruction and guided practice has been provided, the activity tests a student's ability to use new information before skill proficiency has been established.

Application or facilitated practice activities are often confused with explicit teaching or teacher-led instruction and testing. Just because a teacher provides a short overview of expectations and reviews directions for completing an activity, that is not sufficient exposure for students to work independently. The distinction among teaching, facilitated practice, and testing is important as it relates to best practices of expert teaching and high performing schools that achieve significant gains in student performance.

The distinct difference in teaching, facilitated practice, and testing is this: Teaching includes immediate constructive feedback by a teacher or capable peer while students are learning or operating with new information. Facilitated practice happens when students are working with minimal or no support or feedback available. Testing occurs when students are expected to perform before sufficient instruction has occurred. Providing more teaching and improving the quality of the instruction will create significant positive changes in student outcomes and develop highly effective educational programs. That is a common practice found in successful schools.

ALIGNING PERFORMANCE WITH COMMON TRAITS OF HIGHLY SUCCESSFUL SCHOOLS

Reviewing the literature on differentiated instruction reveals a parallel between best practices for effective instruction and the common traits of highly successful schools (FCRR, 2006). Most articles or books written about differentiated instruction use these traits to describe how it should be provided. The materials discuss ways to adjust teaching or modify assignments based on a general conceptual understanding about students' needs. Schools noted for closing the achievement gap and sustaining gains put these traits into action. Highly successful schools demonstrate how to make differentiated instruction occur by actively applying the following traits:

- Establishing strong leadership with clearly defined goals
- Creating collaborative relationships through teaching teams and professional development, including coaching and support
- Developing teacher attitudes and behaviors that support using a management system to organize how instruction occurs in classrooms
- Developing a systemwide attitude toward the effective use of data to align instruction to need, to match text to reader, and to ensure student success
- Developing a systemwide attitude that student collaboration and coaching by teachers and peers is essential for change and for learning of new information, routines, and procedures
- Conceptualizing instruction as modeling, teaching, and repeated practice opportunities with positive constructive feedback

- Envisioning an atmosphere where students work collaboratively with peers providing constructive feedback when teacher support is unavailable

- Envisioning an instructional pace that ensures sufficient teaching has occurred before students work independently on assignments

- Prioritizing and monitoring instructional effectiveness so teachers spend more time teaching and less time facilitating practice, or monitoring students as they complete written assignments or participate in games

Developing Skills Sets for Effective Instruction

Highly successful educational programs focus on improving the quantity and quality of instruction. Professional development is used to help teachers know how to teach and what to teach. Teachers develop effective methods for delivering instruction to ensure two things: more teaching and learning occurs, and students have more opportunities to respond and receive constructive feedback. Improving instructional methodology is critically important. Changes must be made to improve instructional delivery and create supportive learning environments that are learner friendly. There are many ways to achieve these goals:

- Select assessments appropriate to purpose: screening, diagnostic, monitoring progress, and evaluating outcome.

- Use data to determine what students know, what they need, and what they can do.

- Make instructional decisions based on multiple data points and criteria such as students' background knowledge, readiness, language preferences, and learning preferences for activities or guided practice.

- Set expectations for performance so teaching is learner-friendly and flexible to student needs and schedules.

- Provide skills-focused, systematic, explicit instruction in specific skills and knowledge essential to comprehension.

- Use data to group students for instruction.

- Select skills-focused materials and practice activities that are sensitive to student variance, academically profitable, and scaffolded from easy to difficult.

- Provide more intensive intervention for students who continue to struggle by increasing their instructional time, decreasing their group size, or improving the quality and specificity of instruction with more opportunities for reteaching and guided practice.

- Monitor progress, analyze patterns of error, and provide constructive feedback and additional practice specific to need.

- Ensure students receive instruction that prepares them for successfully completing district, state, and national performance goals as measured by state or national assessments. (Elbaum et al., 1998; Elbaum et al., 2000; Foorman & Torgesen, 2001; Hall, 2002; Tomlinson, 1995; Tomlinson & Eidson, 2003; Vaughn et al., 2001).

- Participate in professional development that clarifies how to accomplish these objectives, including actively defining what should occur and how to make it happen in classrooms. Teachers must build effective instructional delivery skill sets based on data that reveals what their students can do, what they need, and what they have to accomplish according to district, state, and national standards.

Developing Environments to Enhance Differentiating Instruction

Some changes may be needed to create an environment that allows small group, differentiated instruction. Attitudes about teaching and changes in delivery styles may also be required to enhance instructional effectiveness and differentiation. The following key points may be helpful to guide discussions about changes that may need to occur:

- Embrace an attitude that supports collaborative teaching and learning that encourages students to share, talk, participate in peer-assisted learning experiences, take risks to ask questions, and ask for and receive positive constructive feedback.

- Use whole class and small group lessons for explicit skills-focused instruction with multiple activities happening simultaneously.

- Establish consistency with routines and procedures and develop planned activities for smooth transitions.

- Pace instruction to provide sufficient time for students to process information and practice skills with support before assigning them as independent work.

- Increase student engagement, or opportunity to respond to instruction, by structuring learning situations that provide immediate constructive feedback from a peer when a teacher is unavailable or working with another group.

- Increase cognitive and emotional supports using a variety of strategies to identify words and construct meanings from text. Teach students how to learn, not just what to learn.

- Participate in professional development that helps teachers establish daily schedules and routines and procedures that embrace new ways of delivering instruction by providing 20 minute lessons using whole class and small groups. Change the way instruction occurs using shorter instructional time periods.

CLARIFYING TEACHER EXPECTATIONS AND REQUIREMENTS

Today, teacher roles in regular education classrooms are more challenging due to increasing student variance and the inclusion of students with special needs. Teaching differently to accommodate the diversity in classrooms may appear as a new concept or expectation for practice, but differentiating instruction to meet the special needs of some students has occurred in classrooms for quite some time. Gifted and talented programs have used data to select and group students for special instruction and engage them in learning activities and projects for nearly two decades (Tilly, 2003; Tomlinson, 2000). Most of the gifted and talented special instruction was provided as a pull-out activity with a special service provider or teacher responsible for the lessons.

Currently, teachers are expected to diagnostically and prescriptively teach all the students in their class. They must develop skill sets that help them differentiate instruction by modifying classroom environments, behaviors, and instruction. This type of differentiation is not simple; it is a constant and complex challenge, even for master teachers. Teachers need tools that help them manage instruction and satisfy instructional demands. They need instruction management so opportunities for effective teaching and positive learning outcomes occur.

DEVELOPING AN INSTRUCTION MANAGEMENT SYSTEM

Teachers readily admit they struggle with instruction management or how to teach using whole class and small group differentiated instruction. Two questions most frequently asked by teachers involve management concerns. Teachers want to know: (1) how they are supposed to get everything done and (2) what the rest of their students are doing when they are working with a small group.

A management system creates routines and procedures that simplify instructional delivery and help teachers use resources efficiently and effectively. In order to utilize a management system, teachers need professional development that provides teachings tools for: (1) collecting and using data for diagnostic decision making about placement in curricula, grouping students for instruction, and monitoring student progress or evaluating achievement; (2) making decisions for selecting teaching strategies, materials, and activities that attend to student variance and are skills focused and academically profitable; and (3) using flexible grouping practices and patterns for managing whole class and small groups to differentiate instruction and enhance student progress and achievement.

Management tools help teachers adjust pacing by alternating time periods for whole class and small group lessons. Establishing routines and procedures is necessary to ensure that every student has daily exposure to teacher-led instruction. This is one hallmark of a successful teaching. Many teachers need professional development, coaching, and support so they can efficiently manage whole class and small group instruction. These tools support teachers and create opportunities for grouping and differentiating instruction: a daily schedule, a job chart, and a rotation chart. Teachers use these tools to differentiate instruction and get everything done. Tools are explained in detail in subsequent chapters.

CHAPTER SUMMARY

Differentiating instruction in response to increasing student variance requires teaching differently by alternating time periods for whole class and small group lessons. Many traits of high performing schools align with critical elements for differentiating instruction: using data to determine students' knowledge and needs, grouping students for instruction, monitoring progress and achievement, and using skills-focused curricula and practice activities that are academically profitable.

Multiple resources are available for assessing or modifying lessons and materials. Management tools for implementing whole class and small group instruction appear to be less common. Teachers need to develop expertise in instruction management so they can create classroom environments that include data-informed, teacher-led, and student-directed whole class and small group learning activities. They must have tools to manage simultaneous activities to get everything done. Establishing clear and consistent routines and procedures is essential to success. Teachers need management tools to deliver effective instruction: (1) a daily schedule that includes time periods for whole class and small group instruction, (2) a job chart for delegating classroom responsibilities to students, and (3) a rotation chart that guides students through activities and teaches organizational planning and decision making.

RESOURCES THAT HELP

http://teachers.net/4blocks/
Provides information on Four Blocks, a multilevel method using the four popular approaches to teaching reading.

www.teach-nology.com/litined/dif_instruction
Uses technology to inform teachers about current practices, literature, and professional development. Additionally, links to a variety of articles including research on educational practices and differentiated instruction are provided.

www.ferr.org/
Florida Center for Reading Research

www.tea.state.tx.us
Texas Education Agency, Click on "Teacher Toolbag." This Web site has many teacher resources and references for student activities and research.

CHAPTER 2

Assessment and Data Management

TEACHERS BECOME DATA-INFORMED BY COLLECTING AND USING MANY kinds of information to make instructional decisions. This chapter suggests nonintrusive ways to integrate assessment with instruction and establish baseline data for students. The data may be used to group students, select materials and activities, and deliver instruction. This chapter does not examine individual assessment tools or describe how to use data from specific assessments. Excellent resources are available online and from publishers that provide teachers with that information (Florida Center for Reading Research, www.fcrr.org; Fountas & Pinnell, 1996; Hall, 2004; Tomlinson, 2000a; Tomlinson & Eidson, 2003; Tyner & Green, 2004; Vaughn & Linan-Thompson, 2004).

Successfully differentiating instruction begins and ends with a clear understanding of students' capabilities as defined by their current skill performance and what they need to do, as defined by district and state standards. Observing and assessing student performance helps teachers understand what to teach and where to begin instruction. Analyzing patterns of error on written assignments or work samples is also helpful for decision making. Developing a system for integrating assessment with instruction and managing paperwork is important for four reasons: (1) data identifies student variance, (2) it helps teachers align instruction to needs, (3) it informs practice to enhance learning, and (4) it is useful for reporting progress and achievement.

DATA AND PAPER MANAGEMENT

Most school systems have adopted standards and schedules for collecting assessment data. Some assessments are administered at the beginning, middle, and end of the year, and some are used to monitor students' progress at preset intervals, that is, reporting periods ending every 6–9 weeks. Collecting informal data during instruction provides helpful information collected in authentic settings.

Most teachers are natural data collectors, and they perform informal assessment tasks automatically when they work with students. Teachers observe, listen, and think about what is working or needs modification. Often teachers adjust instruction based on their interactions with students, but charting their observations or recording modifications to inform their practice often does not occur. Many teachers report they do not have time to accomplish those tasks. However, informal assessment data collected in authentic teaching situations can help teachers make important diagnostic and prescriptive decisions.

There are several ways for teachers to informally collect and analyze data during instruction to determine next steps for skills-focused teaching. First, teachers should think about their purpose for collecting data and how that data will be used. The data helps them identify how to teach students as well as what to teach.

Collecting Data While Teaching and from Work Samples

At first collecting data from observations during small group instruction may sound overwhelming. Actually the process of simultaneously thinking about teaching skills and assessing comprehension ensures instruction is aligned with outcomes. Before you begin to assess a skill, it is important to select an activity that allows students to demonstration the skills you want to observe. You may want to choose an activity that allows more discussion so you can listen and analyze students' thinking before assigning a written assignment. Closely observing students' task approach helps you estimate feelings of confidence. You can determine if sufficient instruction has been provided by judging how quickly students begin working on an assignment and complete it with minimal support. Listening to students' comments and questions helps you determine who needs more help and what kind of help is needed. The following suggestions are helpful for data collection:

- Observe student performance to determine what students know and need.

- Observe student responses to different activities and determine what works best for instruction, whole class or small group activities, and whether students benefit most from collaborative experiences with peer support or working independently.

- Closely monitor to assess students as they apply skills and perform an assignment, providing support as needed.

- Analyze patterns of error based on multiple data points from observations.

- Observe performance on assignments that are directly linked to classroom instruction, and determine if students understand your expectations for performance and have acquired the skills needed to complete the activity.

- Observe often and aggregate data from multiple sources, including informal observations, work samples, and formal assessments, to make summative decisions about progress and achievement.

Setting a Purpose for Collecting Data   Listing a purpose for assessment helps you remain consistent and focused when working with each small group. The purpose for collecting data in small groups is to monitor student progress and determine if adjustments are needed for instruction or changes are needed in curriculum or grouping patterns. If you are planning to test students for mastery on particular skills, you may want to informally assess students using those skills in small group so that constructive feedback may be provided before final assessment occurs. To help focus assessment opportunities:

- Determine the purpose of assessment by identifying specific skill(s) to be observed.

- Determine which students will be observed, when they will be observed, and how they will be observed, in a small group or individually.

- Identify a baseline for acceptable performance, or what defines mastery for that skill at that specific time of introduction, practice, or development.

- Model and review the concept or skill to clarify your expectations.

- Provide students multiple opportunities to demonstrate skills independently.

Charting Observational Comments on Mailing Labels   You can use standard adhesive mailing labels clipped to a clipboard to chart observational comments. Individual comments may or may not be written for every student. Use the following steps to write positively stated comments that summarize your observations or identify student needs.

- Write the purpose of the observation on the first mailing label to maintain focus for assessment or progress monitoring.

- Use one label per student to be assessed. Write each student's name or initials on a label and add the date of the observation.

- Write positively stated comments on each label to summarize individual student performance or identify needs for additional instruction.

- Later, peel off each mailing label and attach it to a separate sheet of paper. File each student's paper with the mailing label in his/her mailbox. The process is similar to maintaining running records, only the teacher is using mailing labels to capture and store comments. Each label becomes a data point used to assess student progress over time.

- Use the comments to plan lessons, select materials and activities, group students for instruction, and monitor progress.

Charting observational comments cannot be intrusive to instruction. The behavior for observing and charting comments occurs as if teachers are making a quick note to themselves on a notepad. The mailing labels must be easily accessible. Keep a clipboard with mailing labels near the teaching table. As students interact, observe their work habits and skills, and chart comments. During a small group instruction, the last few minutes provide an excellent opportunity for you to ask questions and determine students' understanding of the content or concept that was taught or practiced. You should listen to and chart comments on labels, using one for each student assessed that day.

Comments written on the labels are tremendously important to students, too. Sharing the purpose for charting observations helps students feel supported. When they learn that you are collecting information that will be used to improve decision making about their specific needs, students will dictate what to write on the mailing labels. Recalling a personal experience, a young elementary student once told me during a summer school remediation class, "Teacher, write down that I need help with times and I don't mean times like on a clock." He was requesting help with multiplication facts.

Writing Positive, Personalized, and Proactive Comments

It is important to write positively stated comments on the mailing labels. The comments need to communicate your desire to provide meaningful instruction for each student. The comments are kept in student mailboxes so many eyes may have access to them. Writing supportive, helpful comments to direct instruction or compliment progress is informative to other teachers working with a student. Parents are encouraged to read the comments too. Or you may write a summary statement about a student's progress on a report card using your comments. The following suggestions may be helpful for writing comments about observations:

- Use positive words and present tense verbs: *Sam blends /ĕ/ words.*
- Use specific language that communicates what the student needs: *Joe needs help with spelling CVC words.*
- Use specific language to chart success: *Wow! Ian learned to blend CVC words using /ă/ and /ŏ/.*
- Write personal comments in the presence of each student, then read and share your comments with the student to build trusting relationships.
- Read your comments to students before filing it in their portfolio or mailbox. Ask for their input or suggestions to discuss, compliment, and encourage student progress.
- Review comments periodically with individual students and encourage them to make comments about their progress and achievement. Help students set goals using the data that has been collected.

CREATING MAILBOXES FOR DATA AND PAPER MANAGEMENT

Teachers save instructional time by developing a system for data and paper management. They can create order by establishing consistent routines and procedures for managing papers such as homework assignments, report cards or assessments, or general communications such as newsletters shared between school and home. The system works best when it is applied as a standard across all grade levels on a campus. Students learn how to be responsible and accountable and to perform the school behaviors a teacher desires. Students develop organizational behaviors using routines for bringing papers to school, taking them home, and submitting papers or assignments for review.

Papers, assignments, notes, or other forms of communication are kept in the mailboxes, which are created using standard hanging file folders. You can organize the mailboxes by printing students' first or last names on each one and placing them in alphabetical order in a plastic file box. Every student, teacher, or paraprofessional has a mailbox with her/his name on it. Everyone develops the routine of checking her/his mailbox daily upon entry and departure from the classroom. All assignments and papers originate from and are returned to the mailboxes. The mailboxes become a filing system that helps students organize information and develop responsible organizational skills.

Establishing Routines for Paper Management

Teaching students the expectations for paper management saves instructional time and helps students keep their work organized. Creating procedures for paper management has many advantages:

- Students become more accountable for their work and responsible for submitting assignments on time.
- Students learn to organize materials, assignments, lunch money, report cards, etc., in one place for easy retrieval and use.
- Students learn to file incomplete or complete assignments in one place for continued work or completion as homework or for teacher review.
- Students learn the importance of establishing routines for responsibly handling important documents such as work assignments.

You should model how students are expected to deposit mail in mailboxes upon entering the classroom, or prior to and immediately following small group lessons. Students learn to check their mailboxes before leaving the classroom to collect assignments that may need completing at home. Mailboxes become the "in and out" process for storage and paper management. Often teachers create and use two kinds of mailboxes for each student, a public and a private mailbox.

Developing Public Mailboxes

Public mailboxes are located in the classroom where students can easily access them without interrupting instruction. Students, parents, and teachers working with a particular student have free access to the public mailboxes. Each student's mailbox becomes a safe holding place for important documents or work assignments rather than using a notebook or a desk. Materials kept in a public mailbox can include

- notes to or from the teacher, parent, or legal guardian;
- assessments and reports that need to be sent home or have been returned to school;
- worksheets or workbook pages that are incomplete or need to be graded or examined by a peer or teacher to determine student progress;
- work samples that demonstrate progress during a 1–2 week period; and
- mailing label comments from teacher observations.

During transitions between whole class and small group activities, students deposit work in or select materials from their public mailbox. It is helpful to assign one or two students to serve as Mailbox Monitors who distribute and collect the mailboxes as needed during transitions. The Mailbox Monitors help students follow the pretaught procedures for using the mailboxes and ensure that all mailboxes are returned to the file box after use. Use these steps to model and help students understand your expectations for using mailboxes:

- Demonstrate how to gather or deposit materials to/from the mailbox.
- Teach students how to organize papers in the mailbox by placing the materials in chronological order with the most recent work in the front.
- Teach students how to organize papers and review their work and progress at the end of each week, then staple the papers and send them home.
- Demonstrate how to respectfully request and receive assistance from a Mailbox Monitor.

You can save some work samples and use them to monitor progress over time. Those assignments, along with other assessments, can be stored in private mailboxes that are not available for public use.

Using Private Mailboxes

Private mailboxes are used only by the teacher, an administrator, or a parent/guardian. Personal and confidential information is stored in private mailboxes. Each student has a private mailbox that is stored in a location with restricted access. Private mailboxes are NOT located near the public mailboxes. Assessment reports, work samples that reflect progress over time, or materials used to evaluate progress or achievement can be filed in the private mailbox and used in conferences to report student progress. Assignments collected in the private mailboxes can be attached to report cards to demonstrate student performance and progress. At the end of the year, some information from private mailboxes can be collected in a folder that is forwarded to the next year's teacher so that instruction is purposeful at the beginning of a new year.

Assigning Mailbox Monitors

You can assign one or more students to serve as Mailbox Monitors, who help teachers track completion of assignments. Each monitor will need a clipboard with a list of students' names on it. When checking the mailboxes for assignments that are due, the monitor can place a checkmark beside each student's name to indicate which ones completed an assignment and placed it in their mailbox. It may be helpful to follow these steps and create routines performed by Mailbox Monitors. Their duties may include the following:

- Collecting the "mail" or papers from the mailboxes each morning and filing them in a designated location such as the teacher's mailbox.

- Filing individual worksheets in the mailboxes at the end of each day or before class each morning so worksheets are easily accessible for daily assignments. Students can request assistance from the Mailbox Monitor, who retrieves their mailbox for them, if needed. Each student selects assigned worksheets from their mailbox and completes them during workstations. The students return their work to the mailbox as instructed, either at the end of a work period or at the end of the day. Some papers can be returned the next morning if the worksheet was completed as homework. A Mailbox Monitor checks to confirm assignments are placed in the mailbox when students enter or depart from the classroom.

- Checking for materials that must be completed by a designated time or returned to school.

USING DO/DONE FOLDERS TO ORGANIZE STUDENTS' DAILY WORK

Some teachers create a daily folder that remains on each student's desk during the instructional period. This folder can be called a "Do/Done Folder." It holds assignments that need to be completed, incomplete assignments that are works in progress, and completed work that a teacher needs to review.

A pocket-type folder can be used to create a Do/Done Folder. Open the folder and print "Do" on the left pocket of the folder and "Done" on the right pocket. Assignments that students have not started or that are works in progress are filed in the left pocket marked "Do." As students complete each assignment, they file the paper in the right pocket marked "Done." You can check on a student's progress simply by walking by the desk and opening the folder. Designate a place for students to turn in the folders at the end of the class period or day so work is easily retrievable for review. Do/Done Folders help both teachers and students monitor progress and complete assignments on time.

CHAPTER SUMMARY

Collecting and using data are essential for informing decision making. Teachers use data for planning and executing skills-focused instruction, for monitoring progress and evaluating achievement, and for program effectiveness. Many teachers observe and adjust instruction but do not always document their observations. Other teachers may need professional development to help them determine what to observe, chart, and record. Charting observational comments provides valuable informal data points for decision making. Using mailing labels to capture positively stated comments about students' performance helps teachers integrate assessment with instruction and determine next steps. Using public and private mailboxes helps teachers and students create a systematic procedure for data and paper management. Teachers can assign students to serve as Mailbox Monitors, who help other students organize papers and assignments in their mailboxes.

RESOURCES THAT HELP

www.eduref.org/cgi-bin/res.cgi/Evaluation#Organizations
Provides links to articles detailing academic standards and research surrounding assessment, as well as methods for alternative assessment and testing.

http://reading.uoregon.edu/assessment/dibels.php
Discusses the DIBELS (Dynamic Indicators of Basic Early Literacy Skills)
Assessment. The assessment description, essential features, and how and
why to use it in the classroom are addressed.

http://dibels.uoregon.edu/dibels_what.php
Has a detailed resource defining DIBELS and which skills DIBELS assesses;
also includes video clips of what established readers look like.

http://reading.uoregon.edu/assessment/admin_and_scoring6.pdf#search=
'Dynamic%20Indicators%20of%20Early%20Literacy%20skills
Shows an actual DIBELS scoring guide that assesses letter naming fluency,
initial sound fluency, nonsense word fluency, and instructional
recommendations.

www.fcrr.org/assessment/PDFfiles/ParentBrochure.pdf#search='Dynamic%20
Indicators%20of%20Early%20Literacy%20skills
Is a parent's guide to DIBELS that puts this assessment in an easy-to-
understand format.

CHAPTER 3

Grouping for Instruction

EFFECTIVE WAYS TO GROUP STUDENTS FOR SKILLS-FOCUSED INSTRUCTION are critical to differentiating instruction. Grouping patterns and practices are discussed here so that teachers can incorporate flexible grouping in their daily instruction. Information for determining group sizes and assigning group memberships is included to ensure teachers develop compatible and cooperative small groups whose instruction meets the specific needs of each student assigned to a group.

Grouping students for instruction creates opportunities for differentiating instruction, increasing opportunities for student responses, and addressing student variance. Research indicates that students with and without learning disabilities benefit from instruction that encourages them to personally engage, actively participate, and internalize their learning (Elbaum et al.,1998). Maheady (1997) referred to grouping as one of the alterable instructional factors that can powerfully influence the levels of individual student engagement and hence positively affect academic progress.

Grouping practices that enhance reading acquisition skills for students with learning disabilities need to be implemented (Lyon, 1995). Numerous resources and excellent research are available that identify best practices for grouping, explicit and systematic instruction, selecting curriculum, monitoring progress, and evaluating achievement (Farrell, Hancock, & Smart, 2002; Fuchs, Fuchs, Mathes, & Simmons,1997; Gerstein, Vaughn, Deshler, & Schiller, 1997; Hall, 2004; Moody et al., 1997; Vaughn, Hughes, Moody, & Elbaum, 1998; Tomlinson & Eidson, 2003; Tyner, 2004.) Many of these research findings and resources are included in this book.

Critical components for effective implementation of grouping practices to enhance student achievement have been identified in the research (Vaughn, Hughes, Moody, & Elbaum, 2001). Teachers present a lesson, then observe and monitor student progress while providing constructive feedback as needed. Closer observation in small groups and more active engagement improves learning and infuses informal assessment into instruction. Research supports that students learn more in small groups (Elbaum et al., 2000). Yet the emphasis on small group reading instruction as an agent for improving instructional practices and elevating student outcomes has been met with minimal changes in practice and professional development (Come & Fredericks, 1995; Johnson & Johnson, 1975; Labo & Teele, 1990; Moody et al., 1997; Slavin, 1983.)

Regardless of the grade, teachers identify whole class instruction as the system for delivering reading instruction more often than teaching with small groups

(Adadzi, 1985; Barr & Dreeben, 1991; Elbaum, Schumm, & Vaughn, 2000; McIntosh, Vaughn, Schumm, Haager, & Lee, 1993; Slavin, 1987; Tomlinson, 1999; Vaughn et al., 2001). Despite the fact that small group skills-focused instruction has been found to be one of the shared characteristics of the most effective schools for primary grade reading instruction, educational practice is slow to change (Taylor, 2001). Reading instruction offered to students in many schools is not fully utilizing the current research about effective reading practices (Carnine, 1997; Gersten et al., 1997).

GROUPING PRACTICES AND PATTERNS

Teachers need to understand the difference in grouping practices, using whole class or small groups for instruction, and grouping patterns, using homogenous (similar skill) or heterogeneous (mixed skill) groupings. Data informs teachers' decision making about which grouping practice or pattern will be used. Decisions about grouping practices are easier to make than those about grouping patterns. You should select grouping practices, that is, whether to teach the lesson in whole class or small groups, based on

- the purpose of instruction (introduction of content and modeling of expectations, pre-teach vocabulary, or quick practices involving previously taught skills),

- the importance of content (for general knowledge or for explicit skills that are critical to student progress), and

- how much time is available that day for instruction, practice, or review.

Everything can be introduced, modeled, practiced, or reviewed in whole class. You can use partners or unison responses to engage students, but that is differing delivery, not instruction. When the whole class learns the same thing, instruction is not differentiated. It can represent a different way of teaching with more student engagement, but the teacher is still teaching everyone the same thing. Whole class grouping practices work for overview-type instruction or guided practice using peers for feedback. But information that is critical for student achievement needs to be re-presented and taught in small groups. Teachers need to provide data-informed, explicit skills-focused instruction to assist individual students in small groups.

Using small groups allows teachers to personalize and individualize lessons so that each student benefits. Teachers often say their students cannot hide in small groups. Close observation of student performance and opportunities to observe error patterns allow teachers to really notice and monitor student needs. Once teachers listen to individual students discuss, read text, or apply skills in a small group setting, they are sold on small group instruction. Often teachers report that they know their students better than before and they teach more than they ever thought possible using small groups.

Teachers use small group instruction when they need to ensure students understand what is taught, and they can observe students using the information to perform as expected. Skills that are critically important for mastery must be taught and practiced in small groups under the close supervision of a skillful teacher. Positive, immediate constructive feedback must be available to help students efficiently and effectively learn and achieve. Observing student responses on a personal level in a small group helps teachers know when assignments using newly introduced skills can be used in other settings, either students working in workstations or independently at their desks.

How teachers choose to group their students for instruction involves decisions about grouping patterns. Teachers can use homogeneous (similar skill groupings) or heterogeneous (mixed skill groupings). Deciding which grouping patterns will be used depends on

- data that informs teachers about what students know, can do, and need;

- observations of student behaviors that indicate which students will work together cooperatively;

- the purpose of instruction (introduction, practice, enrichment, assessment) and expectation for mastery or change in student performance; and

- what activity will be used to most efficiently and effectively accomplish the instructional goal. Some activities are more meaningfully taught in small groups because the level of difficulty is so high that students need more attention and support.

Teachers use data to select grouping patterns. They assign students to small groups that will work together and allow teachers to present instruction in learner-friendly ways, that is, whole class, small groups, partnering, and working independently (Tomlinson & Eidson, 2003). Data-informed grouping helps teachers deliver more effective differentiated instruction. Grouping students for instruction based on direct measurement and analysis of student performance is becoming more prevalent in classrooms. Mixing skill levels within small groups using high/medium and medium/low skill groupings is effective for teacher-led instruction and guided practice. However, some skills or instructional purposes (assessment) can be more efficiently and effectively accomplished with similar skill grouping patterns. The key to successful grouping is flexibility and using what works to achieve the instructional purpose. Teachers use grouping practices and patterns that maximize the use of instructional time to increase student achievement.

Improving Student Outcomes with Small Group Instruction

Teachers enhance students' learning using instructional conversations that are easier to conduct and support in small groups (Goldenberg, 1993). The responsibility for instruction and learning is shared between the teacher and the students. There are numerous advantages to using small group skills-focused instruction:

- Teachers form a more personal relationship with each student.

- Teachers gain a deeper understanding of individual variances and needs for modifications.

- Teachers are more informed and equipped for decision making, planning, and teaching.

- Students receive better instruction because the teacher observes error patterns and provides immediate constructive feedback.

- Students have more opportunities to express what they know and receive feedback from other students.

- Students are more engaged and have more opportunities for responding and applying information.

VARYING GROUPING PATTERNS USING SIMILAR OR MIXED SKILL GROUPS

A typical class is comprised of students whose skill levels span several years. Students can be grouped by skill level using homogeneous or heterogeneous pairings. Each type has distinct advantages and disadvantages, and neither should be used exclusively. Effective instruction includes using the grouping practice that aligns with multiple tiers of instructional support to assist struggling learners. Many resources are available that help teachers align their grouping practices with effective reading instruction (Hall, 2004; Vaughn, 2003). References are provided at the end of this chapter for those who want to read more about grouping for the instructional tiers needed for both response to intervention (RTI) and the Three-Tier Model for reading instruction (www.tea.org).

Grouping Students Homogenously

Homogeneous skill groupings are excellent for students who need intensive intervention for reading skills (Vaughn, 2003). Ideally, homogeneous grouping patterns can be used to introduce, practice, or assess specific skills and for intensive intervention, but they are not to be rigid and inflexible or implemented continuously.

Research has criticized homogeneous grouping patterns for lowering self-esteem and motivation, restricting friendships and choices, and widening the gap between high and low achievers. Using similar-skill grouping patterns often creates the scenario where the poorest readers receive poor quality instruction (Abadzi, 1985; Calfee & Brown, 1979; Good & Stipek, 1983; Hiebert, 1983; Kulik,

1992; Labo & Teele, 1990; Rosenholtz & Wilson, 1980; Vaughn et al., 2001). In addition, grouping lower performing students together reduces the availability of a peer who can provide assistance when the teacher is unavailable.

Grouping Students Heterogeneously

Heterogeneous, or mixed skill, groupings provide excellent practice opportunities that incorporate collaboration, shared learning, and peer tutoring with assistance when the teacher is unavailable (Elbaum et al., 1998; Elbaum et al., 2000a; Fountas & Pinnell, 1996; Goldenberg, 1993; Lou et al., 1996). Small groups that combine students with high/medium and medium/low skills appear to work well for peer tutoring. Regrouping using flexible grouping is strongly encouraged in order to include students in smaller mixed level groups that encourage collaboration and peer interactions (Foorman & Torgesen, 2001; Mathes, Denton, Fletcher, Anthony, Francis, & Schatschneider, 2005; Tilly, 2003).

SUBDIVIDING THE WHOLE CLASS INTO SMALLER GROUPS USING PARTNERING

Depending on the students' skill levels, a whole class approach can be useful for the initial introduction of a skill or concept. This includes visually and verbally modeling a lesson. A whole class approach can also be effective for practicing or reviewing a skill that has been attained by everyone to varying degrees. When a new skill is introduced and the teacher has modeled expectations, the whole class can be subdivided into partnerships, trios, or quartets for guided practice.

Grouping students within a whole class session is one way to effectively use flexible grouping. Students grouped within a whole class lesson benefit from increased student engagement, additional repeated practice opportunities and less passive listening. Grouping within a group uses time and space efficiently. Students simply respond to a partner or peer sitting nearby.

A variety of techniques can increase student engagement in whole class sessions:

- Students respond in unison by answering aloud to teacher questions.

- Students respond by signaling, such as, Thumbs Up, Thumbs Down, where students use their thumb to indicate agreement or disagreement to statements made or questions asked by the teacher or other students.

- Students turn to a partner or person sitting beside them and restate a concept, spell a word, or use a vocabulary word in an oral sentence.

- In small groups of 4 or fewer, students discuss a concept or solve a problem collaboratively for a prescribed length of time, perhaps 5–10 minutes. A member from each group then shares the work with the whole group or class.

INCORPORATING FLEXIBLE GROUPING

Changing group memberships according to student achievement, type of activity or skill, or resources (time, equipment, personnel) affects how you differentiate instruction. Flexible grouping has become more popular and alternative grouping practices such as cooperative learning and peer tutoring have developed (Elbaum, Moody, & Schumm, 1999). Flexible grouping and small group reading instruction have substantial scientific research that validates their usefulness for enhancing reading achievement (Elbaum et al., 1998; Foorman & Torgesen, 2001; Fountas & Pinnell, 1996; Fuchs et al., 1997; Hall, 2002; Maheady, 1997). Small group instruction and peer partnering activities have been used successfully to increase student engagement in guided practice activities.

Cooperative groups and peer pairing provide alternatives to whole group, lecture format instruction and provide multiple practice opportunities with constructive feedback (Moody et al., 1997). Flexible grouping allows group memberships to change in response to student needs and avoid the negative stereotyping associated with traditional ability grouping (Calfee & Brown, 1979; Good & Stipek, 1983). Choices of grouping practices and patterns vary according to the skill taught, instructional purpose, and the type of activity used. Decisions about group memberships are critical to successful implementation.

Using Whole Class and Small Group Skills-Focused Lessons

Creating opportunities for flexible grouping can include changing group memberships or selecting specific practices that regulate how small groups will rotate from activity to activity. There are many methods for implementing flexible grouping:

- Change group memberships as data indicates that student needs have changed.
- Select different procedures that regulate how students participate in workstations, such as using a rotation chart to direct "flow," the procedure that students follow to attend workstations and activities for teacher-led instruction.

Table 3.1 outlines grouping practices that can be used to differentiate reading instruction using teacher-directed whole class and small group lessons.

Reassigning Group Memberships as Student Data Indicates

Group memberships need to be compatible and flexible, reflecting what students can do and need. Regrouping should occur as often as achievement data indicates it is needed. Compatibility and availability of peer assistance within each group are always important. Tables 3.2 and 3.3 illustrate one way to use flexible grouping formats. The same 27 students are divided into four small groups for reading instruction in two patterns: homogeneous small groups and heterogeneous pairs for peer tutoring. Depending on the skill or activity to be used, select the grouping format that will be most effective for delivering instruction.

TABLE 3.1

TEACHER-DIRECTED GROUPING ARRANGEMENTS		
GROUP	**INSTRUCTIONAL FOCUS**	**GROUP FORMATION**
Whole Class	• Introduce & model new concepts • Practice concepts not mastered • Review concepts	• All students in class (can use partnering activities to group within whole class)
Small Group	• Instruction that is data-informed & aligned with student-specific needs • Explicit skills instruction	• 4–8 students • Data-informed grouping • Partnering activities can be used
Collaborative Groups (mixed skill sets)	• Practice previously taught concepts • Partnering activities	• Based on students' skills or interests • Peer partners • Small study groups
One-to-One	• Intensive instruction for specific student needs	• Based on assessment data

SELECTING GROUP SIZES

Small group sizes vary according to the skill or activity to be taught, the instructional purpose, and individual student needs. Assess students' skills to determine needs and use the data to inform your decision making for assigning group memberships. In addition, ensure group memberships are compatible so that each small group can work collaboratively with and without your direct supervision.

More research is needed to determine the most effective group sizes and the role of teachers using small group differentiated instruction (Vaughn et al., 2001). Generally students working on or above grade level can be grouped in larger groups of 8–10 students, depending on the skill taught and the type of activity used. When working with students who are struggling, closer supervision is needed to teach toward skill mastery. Providing more opportunities for students to actively respond is critical. Generally, the group size decreases as student needs increase, allowing students to have more practice opportunities for responding and receiving constructive feedback. Smaller groups of 4–6 students are preferred to increase opportunities for student engagement and peer interaction (Elbaum et al., 1999). Smaller teacher-led groups were associated with qualitatively and quantitatively better instruction (Thurlow, Ysseldyke, Wotruba, & Algozzine, 1993). Vaughn and Linan-Thompson (2004) suggest that small groups of 4–6 students can be used to teach specific skills such as phonemic awareness, but students requiring more intense interventions benefit from smaller groups where one teacher works with 1:1, 1:3, or 1:5 students (Vaughn & Chard, 1999).

Smaller group sizes appear to be most effective, but they may not be as efficient. One-to-one instruction is usually impractical. More research is needed to

TABLE 3.2

GROUPING: HOMOGENEOUS/PATTERN: SMALL GROUPS		
GROUP	**STUDENTS**	**COMPETENCY OR SKILL LEVEL**
Group 1	8 students	Reading above grade level
Group 2	8 students	4 students reading fluently on grade level and 4 students who need skill practice and review
Group 3	6 students	Reading on grade level; need skill review; approaching grade level
Group 4	5 students	Low performing, reading below grade level

TABLE 3.3

GROUPING: HETEROGENEOUS/PATTERN: PARTNERED PEER TUTORING		
GROUP	**STUDENTS**	**COMPETENCY OR SKILL LEVEL**
Group 1	8 students	4 students reading above grade level and 4 students reading fluently approaching grade level, needing skill review
Group 2	6 students	3 students reading fluently on grade level and 3 students reading on grade level, needing skill review
Group 3	8 students	4 students reading above grade level and 4 students approaching or on grade level
Group 4	5 students	5 students who are approaching grade level or reading below grade level, working with teacher in pairs of 2–3 students each

determine the effectiveness of one-to-one and one-to-three grouping patterns. Using such small groups reduces instructional time for all students and increases documentation and paperwork for teachers. Smaller group sizes can be time-consuming, which impedes services to all students and utilizes teacher time for planning and preparing for instruction (Vaughn et al., 2001). Simply put, when a teacher forms too many small groups, each group receives less teacher-led instruction time.

Optimum Group Sizes

Teachers usually create three to four small groups with approximately 4–8 students per group. More intense instruction in smaller groups of 1–3 students may be used to allow more opportunities for participation, questions, and feedback (FCRR, 2006; Vaughn & Linan-Thompson, 2004; Vaughn et al., 2001).

In order to create optimum group sizes, you should

- use data to select the skill to be learned or activity used for practice,
- assess the number of previous exposures to skill to determine if lessons will be introduction of skill or review with guided practice,

- determine the level of student mastery required at that time of instruction, that is, larger group sizes can be used for review and guided practice,

- evaluate instructional resources available, such as time, personnel, and curriculum materials,

- chart the time allowed for instruction, for example, 1 hour or 90–120 minutes,

- select the amount of content or the skills that will be taught during a specific time, that is, instructional purpose and goal,

- determine the supervision needed to make the activity academically profitable and successful, that is, students' skills and capabilities to work with or without teacher support or supervision to achieve the task, and

- take the number of students who will participate during a specific period and determine how many groups can be formed and taught during that time, that is, in 1 hour with 28 students, only two groups can spend 20–25 minutes each in teacher-led small group instruction.

You should determine which grouping pattern works best for introducing a new concept or skill, practicing a previously taught skill, or working independently. Highly focused and well-sequenced lessons maximize the use of instructional time in any group size. In order to assign group memberships effectively,

- calculate the total number of students that you will work with during your instructional period, that is, 26 students in class for reading instruction,

- calculate the amount of instructional time, that is, you have a 90 minute block to teach reading,

- identify how many small groups can be taught based on the time allowed for reading instruction, that is, 3–4 small groups meeting 20 minutes each can be used in 90 minute reading blocks, with 10 minutes allowed for opening and closing the lesson, and

- determine what activities and materials work best for the skill that will be taught, that is, students can partner allowing you to "group within a large group" and provide more student interaction. Responses can be in unison so larger group sizes can be used. Individual students need to perform or read, so smaller group sizes are required.

You can create more than one kind of grouping pattern. Flexible grouping allows you to change group memberships when the skill, activity, or the academic content changes. Small homogeneous groups can be formed for a particular skill lesson, for example, reading decodable words in connected text. The same students can be regrouped for a partnering activity using mixed ability groups. Group memberships change depending on what students need, what the data reveals about their progress, and how you want to teach or practice a skill. This is true regardless of the area of academic focus—reading, math, or other subject areas.

Student skill levels vary across academic subjects. Usually group memberships differ for reading and math instruction, so grouping students solely on reading achievement is an instructional error. Generally, students who are low performing in reading do not always demonstrate skill weaknesses in math. Group sizes can vary also. Larger groups may be used to teach math and other content areas. You need to use data per content area and group students so that instruction meets their needs.

Grouping for Compatibility and Cooperation

There are a number of ways to ensure compatibility and cooperation within groups:

- Observe students and assign them to groups based on compatibility so that each group works cooperatively or collaboratively without teacher supervision. Students will interrupt the teacher constantly if students with incompatible behaviors are not separated. Students who do not work cooperatively together without supervision need to be assigned to different groups, if possible.

- Assign a leader to serve as coordinator for each small group. Actually, each student is encouraged to self-regulate and monitor, as well as share responsibilities for leadership and assisting others, but the coordinator becomes the leader when issues need resolving.

- Assign students to each group so that the grouping represents a variety of skill levels to encourage peer tutoring and collaboration during practice activities. The goal is to develop collaborative understandings in small study groups to create opportunities for applying skills and having discussions about the activity or skill.

- Teach routines and procedures for working in small groups.

- Discuss, model, and practice ways for group members to request and receive assistance.

- Assign jobs to students in the classroom to develop routines and procedures during transitions.

CHAPTER SUMMARY

Teachers respond to student variance using data from informal and formal assessments to group students, improve instruction, increase engagement, and enhance student achievement. Grouping practices play a critical role in facilitating effective implementation for reading instruction. Homogeneous or similar skill group-ings are usually used for whole class instruction and are useful for introducing, modeling, demonstrating, and reviewing content or skills. Heterogeneous or mixed skill groupings are useful when teachers need to work closely with students in smaller groups and provide explicit skills instruction with immediate construc-tive feedback. Flexible grouping may be used to increase student engagement, col-laboration, and create opportunities for peer partnering activities. Teachers need routines and procedures for organizing the classroom environment and manag-ing whole class and small group instruction. Establishing order in the classroom enhances student participation and successful achievement.

RESOURCES THAT HELP

Fountas, I. C., & Pinnell, G. S. (1996). *Guided reading: Good first teaching for all children*. Portsmouth, NH: Heinemann.

Tomlinson, C. A., & Eidson, C. C. (2003). *Differentiation in practice: A resource guide for differentiating curriculum, grades K–5*. Alexandria, VA: Association for Supervision and Curriculum Development.

Tyner, B. (2004). *Small-group reading instruction: A differentiated teaching model for beginning and struggling readers*. Newark, NJ: International Reading Association.

Vaughn, S. (2003, December). *How many tiers are needed for response to inter-vention to achieve acceptable prevention outcomes?* Paper presented at the National Research Center on Learning Disabilities Responsiveness-to-Intervention Symposium, Kansas City, MO.

Vaughn, S., & Linan-Thompson, S. (2004). *Research-based methods of reading instruction for grades K–3*. Alexandria, VA: Association of Supervision and Curriculum Development.

www.eduref.org/cgi-bin/res.cgi/Evaluation#Organizations
Provides links to articles detailing academic standards and research on assessment as well as methods for alternative assessment and testing.

www.ncrel.org/sdrs/areas/stw_esys/4assess.htm
Describes the purpose of assessing students and the characteristics of quality assessment.

http://ecot.rice.edu/conferences/acpweb/UST/EDUC5325/fluency.html
Provides a video clip of the partner reading technique. The clip explains this strategy in detail and shows how to implement it in the classroom.

www.readingrockets.org/articles/c64
Provides articles detailing information on grouping students for instruction and adapting teaching strategies to meet students' needs.

www.teach-nology.com/tutorials/teaching/differentiate/planning/
Provides a look at the benefits of, methods of, and reasons for grouping for instruction in the classroom.

www.nwrel.org/scpd/sirs/1/cu2.html
Includes an article describing why instructional groups are used, what types are used by teachers, and actions for effectiveness when grouping for instruction.

www.tea.org
Texas Education Agency

www.fcrr.org
Florida Center for Reading Research

CHAPTER 4

Organizing Classrooms and Schedules

TO HELP TEACHERS IMPLEMENT DIFFERENTIATED INSTRUCTION efficiently and effectively in well-managed classrooms, this chapter provides suggestions for organizing classrooms and for managing instruction. It includes research-based, field-tested, and validated suggestions that teachers may use to establish routines and procedures and set up their classroom to incorporate whole and small group instruction.

Systematic studies of effective classroom management are relatively recent, and they clearly have importance for implementing differentiating instruction (Marzano, 2003). Teachers need procedures that help them maximize the use of instructional time. Providing explicit instruction in small groups and managing students working in other activities can be a perplexing problem for teachers. Frequently they ask, "What are the rest of my students doing while I am working with a small group?" Getting organized to teach begins with sharing the work in the classroom by assigning jobs to students.

ASSIGNING JOBS IN THE CLASSROOM COMMUNITY

Teachers use instructional time more efficiently by delegating some of the classroom duties and responsibilities to students. Sharing jobs in the classroom community teaches students an important life skill, that is, when you live in a community, you share the work. If you work in a community, then you will be held accountable for your work and responsibilities.

Students learn from the leadership opportunities when they work collaboratively with their peers and make decisions using appropriate language and word choices that honor contributions of other classmates. They learn to assist others and compliment collaborative efforts when others cooperate. They develop a sense of community and collaboration by participating in assigned jobs. They become more responsible and accountable while using language to cooperate and solve problems.

Assigning students to complete jobs helps you, too. Sharing the responsibilities with students allows you to focus on instruction, not classroom management. Students assist others and help organize and clean up work areas in the classroom before and after each activity. One or more students can be assigned as monitors responsible for checking workstations or the worktable. Checking the work areas

FIGURE 4.1
A sample job chart

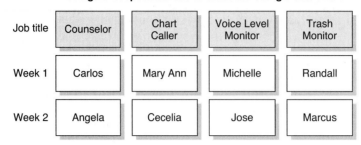

Delegate Responsibilities to Students Using a Job Chart

Job title	Counselor	Chart Caller	Voice Level Monitor	Trash Monitor
Week 1	Carlos	Mary Ann	Michelle	Randall
Week 2	Angela	Cecelia	Jose	Marcus

Teach important life skills:

• If you live in a community, you share responsibilities/work.
• If you work in the community, you will be held accountable for your work.

provides something for students to do during transitions. Through meaningful work, students learn how to appreciate and compliment the contributions of their peers and understand the influence that they have on their environment.

Jobs used in classrooms will vary according to grade level, student capabilities, and teacher needs. Creating a job chart helps you delegate responsibilities in the classroom community and ensures that all students participate in leadership. Create a job chart to communicate expectations and help students remember their responsibilities for the week. See Figure 4.1 and the accompanying photo.

Use these suggestions to develop a job chart and delegate responsibilities to students:

- Begin by listing every duty you do that is not explicit teaching (organizing papers, checking supplies, checking the classroom for clutter, checking student work assignments, etc.).

- Use a highlighter and mark the jobs on your list that can be assigned to a student.

- Develop a job title for each of those tasks, for example, Trash Monitor, the student assigned to be the watchdog for classroom disorder and clutter.

- Print each job title on a 3-inch X 5-inch index card and add pictures for younger children who cannot read the print.

- Place the job title cards in a pocket chart or use pushpins to post the job title cards in a column on the left side of the bulletin board. Assign fewer jobs at first and add more jobs as students become more responsible.

- Print each student's name on a 3-inch X 5-inch index card and use pictures for support when working with younger students.

- Make job assignments by selecting a student's name and placing that student's name card beside a job title card.

- Select the number of students that will be chosen to work each week. Teachers can assign more than one student per job title, that is, the teacher can assign 2 students to serve as Workstation Monitors during transitions.

- Rotate the student's names at the end of each week to make new assignments and ensure that all students participate.

Teaching Expectations for Classroom Collaboration

During the first week of implementation, discuss expectations, roles, and responsibilities, and train students so they know how to perform each expectation or job. You need to plan time for modeling and demonstrating how to perform each duty, using kind words to request help, providing assistance while honoring the efforts of another student, having patience when guiding others, and showing tolerance when things do not go as planned.

Establishing clear expectations and routines or procedures is essential to success. You need to talk with students and encourage their input about job descriptions and expectations for performance. It is helpful to use students in role-play situations or what-if experiences to practice, model, and teach how to respond to different situations that may arise. Help students develop language skills that include proper word choices and behaviors for assisting others. Students learn the ability to work with others using language and social skills to create a classroom community that communicates respectfully and collaborates cooperatively. That kind of community collaboration creates teaching opportunities using differentiating instruction.

It is critical to model and teach procedures for communication:

- Model how to request help from the teacher or other students.
- Model when to request help or interrupt the teacher or another student for assistance.
- Role-play how to respectfully interrupt someone and gratefully accept help from a peer when the teacher is unavailable.
- Demonstrate and practice how to provide assistance to other classmates using words and behaviors that are constructive and honorable.
- Demonstrate proper word choices and voice tones for requesting or providing assistance and for complementing efforts or achievements.
- Role-play how to demonstrate appreciation by complimenting efforts, not just achievements, and teach students how to receive the compliment.
- Model how to assist with problem solving by discussing issues with others and accepting ideas from others as potential solutions.
- Teach students how to accept and respond to the authority of other students.

The second week of implementation builds on the job skills learned the first week. You now have students from week one train the students for duties in week two. Simply make a second row of names to the right of the student name cards for week one. Provide positive feedback or additional modeling as needed. Later, assign week two students to train week three assignees. Soon, every student has been trained in at least one job, and there have been ample opportunities to observe other students at work. With each successive week, on-the-job training continues in this same way. In fact, it is very interesting to watch students coach each other. They improve their skill sets socially, emotionally, and academically by teaching and helping each other.

The jobs for any classroom community are limited only by your imagination. Some obvious positions are:

- *Chart Caller*   Reads a rotation chart and helps direct students to activities
- *Counselor or Special Friend*   Assists other students in need and helps locate lost items, listens to complaints, and redirects students who need help with decision making
- *Timekeeper*   Monitors use of time in small groups and provides 5 minute warnings before transitions
- *Trash (or Environmental) Monitor*   In charge of supervising and maintaining order in the general classroom environment and assists other students in keeping desks and work areas clean
- *Voice Level Monitor*   Supervises and monitors noise levels in classroom

- *Mailbox Monitor*   Places worksheets in mailboxes, checks for homework or papers that need to be assessed or corrected

- *Workstation Monitor/Center Checker*   Monitors use of workstations and helps students cleanup to make speedy transitions

- *Worktable Monitor*   Checks supplies and area surrounding the worktable

- *Books Monitor*   Selects books as needed to read in whole group or for activities using textbooks or organizes books when used by students in transitions

- *Supply Monitor*   Checks supplies in classrooms and checks in and out supplies that students may need to borrow: pencil, paper, pen, facial tissues, toilet paper, and supplies at special project areas such as art, math, and science workstations

- *Line Leader*   Stands at the front of the line

- *Lights Monitor*   Responsible for turning off the lights

- *Recess Assistant*   Selects and carries items needed for recess or PE

- *Teaching Assistant*   Assists others with assignments at workstations or worktables

- *Teacher Assistant*   Assists you with organizing materials or activity, takes notes to office, or distributes papers

- *Correspondent*   Responsible for listening to, synthesizing, and reporting student's lengthy stories about events that happened recently so as to avoid lengthy dialogue during whole class or small group lessons

Strategically Selecting Students for Jobs the First Week

Some students need and will benefit from explicit modeling during the first week. Assigning specific roles to some students during the first week ensures they get teacher-directed, explicit instruction in areas they need. Match student needs with specific jobs or roles in the community so they benefit from the modeling and explicit instruction. Use these tips to match student needs with jobs:

- *Trash or Environmental Monitor*   Choose a student that needs to develop a skill set for maintaining order or getting organized.

- *Counselor*   Choose a student most likely to tattle or fret, use physical means to solve problems, or who needs to learn graceful tolerance.

- *Timekeeper*   Choose a student most likely to lag behind and not keep pace with instruction, one who needs to work on a schedule.

- *Voice Level Monitor*   Choose a student who uses improper voice tones or word choices.

- *Mailbox Monitor*   Choose one or two students who lack organizational skills or struggle with maintaining routines.

- *Supply Monitor*   Choose a student who frequently misplaces supplies needed for classroom performance.

During the first week, you should overcoach the job responsibilities to the student workers. Extend students' learning about clean-up responsibilities by taking pictures of work areas in the classroom that illustrate your expectations for order and cleanliness, and post classroom pictures on the bulletin board with a sentence strip that says, "This is clean." Monitors are encouraged to reference pictures when determining if a workstation or work area passes inspection for "clean." You should also post pictures on the bulletin board that include students completing jobs and add positive comments to encourage collaboration and cooperation. You need to coach for success and encourage students to give and receive compliments about their performance.

ORGANIZING THE CLASSROOM ENVIRONMENT

Create work areas that engage students and provide active participation while you are teaching a small group. Work areas need to be free of clutter and contain materials to support instruction for one to two activities. Students attend the workstations only 20–30 minutes, so multiple activity choices are unnecessary. You must carefully select activities for workstations and estimate the time required to complete them. If an activity cannot be completed within the time allotted for the workstation, you need to clarify expectations for completing the assignment or filing the papers in the mailbox for completion later.

Effective instructional management involves creating rules and procedures that develop predictable order and safety so students are comfortable taking risks and learning (Marzano, 2003). Tools that will help you organize the classroom include: a job chart for sharing responsibilities in the classroom, a daily schedule that alternates time periods for whole class and small group instruction, and a rotation chart that communicates expectations and guides students through activities. Rotation charts and transitions are discussed in Chapter 5. You need to develop work areas in the classroom and model and teach expectations for their use. Figures 4.2 and 4.3 show two different arrangements.

Designating an Area for a Teaching Table

Select a place in the classroom for teacher-led, skills-focused, small group instruction; that place may be called "the teaching table." It should be located near materials often used for instruction, that is, student books, workbooks, and writing utensils. The largest number of students assigned to a small group dictates the amount of space for a teaching table. If the largest group of students is 8, then space for 8 students and a teacher is required. Sometimes you must be resourceful in creating a teaching table and may need to use one of the following options:

- A designated table as a workspace or a computer station if modeling a lesson using technology

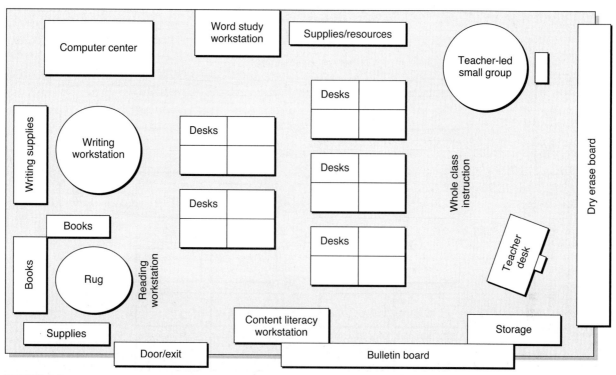

FIGURE 4.2

This room arrangement allows the teacher to store instructional materials in an area located near a dry erase board that is used for student practice activities. Workstations, or learning centers, are located near students' supplies. Student desks may be pushed together to develop work areas, or a work table, where students work collaboratively in small study groups. There are pathways among the stations and desk groupings to allow easy access and movement. There is access to the exit from all locations.

- A designated area located on the floor or rug
- Several desks pushed together to create a workspace
- Chairs organized in a small semi-circle to form a teaching area and clip-boards as a writing surface or table

The teaching table is the place for small group differentiated skills-focused teacher-led instruction. Other students complete assignments at a worktable or workstations. Students participate in small group activities at the teaching table or workstations for approximately 20–30 minutes. Younger students many need 15–20 minute activities. Instruction at the teaching table is reserved for teacher-led activities with immediate constructive feedback from a peer or the teacher. Teaching at the teaching table is on students' instructional skill level. You should NOT expect students to work independently on assignments using new skills taught at the teaching table until sufficient instruction and guided practice has occurred. Direct teacher-student interactions occur at the teaching table, that is, reading aloud so the teacher can monitor fluency and use error analysis to determine student need.

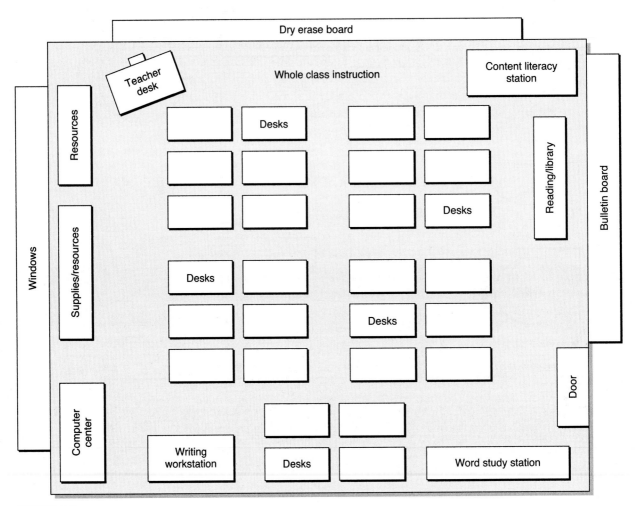

FIGURE 4.3

This arrangement illustrates how to move desks into clusters that may be used for collaborative study groups and workstations or a teaching table or work table for homework activities. Whole group instruction occurs with students sitting at their desks. Independent activities may be completed at desks or workstations. Small group instruction occurs at a desk cluster or table area, or in an assigned place for specific needs such as the computer center. Resources and supplies are located nearby for easy access.

Depending on the daily schedule, students may attend the teaching table twice per day if you have full-day responsibility with the same students. Teacher-directed instruction at the teaching table can occur once each morning and again in the afternoon for additional 20 minute sessions. Reading and language arts instruction usually occurs in the morning and another 20 minute session at the teaching table occurs in the afternoon for math, science, or social studies. Teaching other academic skills in small groups helps extend reading instruction and apply skills in other subject content. Cross-curricular instruction and exposure to skills-focused small group instruction every day, or sometimes twice a day for some students, powerfully improves student achievement.

Designating an Area for a Worktable

Recognizing the need to change traditional practices, teachers should allow some students to begin and possibly complete homework assignments at school together, collaboratively in small groups where help is available, so they do not practice errors. Practice activities, like homework, can be started and perhaps completed at a worktable. A paraprofessional, a parent, or a peer can monitor as students work collaboratively on assignments in small groups. The purpose of the worktable is to allow students to study and work collaboratively with a partner or in small groups to complete practice assignments. A resourceful teacher can configure the classroom to create a worktable with one of the following options:

- Using a designated table that seats 4–8 students
- Pushing 4–6 desks together to create a worktable
- Designating a special rug as the work area and provide clipboards
- Designating a section on the floor for work and provide clipboards

Encouraging Collaboration at Worktables   Stretching former paradigms about copying is needed here. People learn by copying a model. They need to hear, see, say, and do an activity to make it become their behavioral habit. Teachers need to encourage sharing work because it helps students solve problems and work cooperatively to achieve success. Students share their work during practice activities, especially when the skills or concepts have just been introduced. Copying a good example is viewed as helpful instruction and extended teaching. Having students verbalize their thinking and tutor others is viewed as extended instruction because constructive feedback is available.

Working in small collaborative groups that share information and work resembles study groups used in college and collective teamwork used in professional environments. When an activity is NOT going to be assessed or graded, students collaborate and work together to complete assignments. Copying is allowed. The purpose of instruction is to ensure students learn the information and practice with support until they acquire the necessary skills to complete a task. When sufficient instruction has occurred and an assignment will be assessed or graded, then the teacher asks that students work independently at their desks during the time assigned for the worktable. Before asking students to work independently, the teacher ensures sufficient instruction has occurred. Observing students perform at the teaching table provides that information to teachers. They can monitor students' progress closely at the teaching table and thereby know when assignments can be completed independently and assessed for mastery.

Students can begin practice activities or homework assignments at a worktable. This allows students to get help with questions before completing an assignment at home where assistance may not be available. Some teachers voice concerns about students staying on task in small groups at the worktable. Most teachers report their students are more likely to complete their homework successfully at the worktable, or at least a large portion of it, because they have support from their peers. Allowing homework to be started and sometimes completed at school is an incentive for students to remain on task at the worktable. Students feel rewarded for working hard and completing their assignments.

Teachers and paraprofessionals can listen, observe, and monitor the conversations of students as they work at the worktable to assess needs or plan instruction. Much can be learned about students' needs for instruction and their progress depending on the questions asked and the amount of support some individuals need from their peers. You can observe and listen while monitoring classrooms from the teaching table. You can provide feedback when there is an opportunity to leave the teaching table. But, students are expected to complete their work at the worktable with less teacher support and supervision. Later in the day or after school, you can review completed assignments and provide additional constructive feedback, but close teacher supervision does not occur at a worktable. Carefully assigning work at the worktable is needed. You need to select assignments that require minimal teacher support and that offer practice opportunities using previously taught skills introduced and practiced either in the whole class or at the teaching table.

Completing written assignments or group projects are examples of students working on facilitated practice activities at the worktable. The activities are supported by peer collaboration using materials that students access together. Asking students to work independently on materials at a worktable before sufficient instruction has been provided is an instructional error common to many classrooms. Pacing instruction and assigning appropriate activities that provide repeated practice with constructive feedback are essential for successful small group instruction.

Activities at the worktable are practice assignments using skills that have been previously taught AND LEARNED at the teaching table. Preferably students have demonstrated at least 60–70 percent mastery of skills at the teaching table before independent practice is expected at the worktable. Students are encouraged and allowed to work together, providing corrective feedback to one another, so you are not interrupted while teaching another small group. Some teachers assign a worktable monitor to provide assistance as needed, or assign a team leader for each small group.

Some common, and effective, practice activities for the worktable are

- worksheets or workbook pages from the student materials provided with core reading programs,
- answering questions at the end of a story or chapter of a book,
- special project assignments related to current theme or skill,
- spelling or writing assignments,
- research or special project assignments to report on a specific theme or event,
- art materials for creative expression or developing illustrations that align to specific themes, stories, or vocabulary,

- activities for reviewing vocabulary words to enhance word meaning and oral language development,

- homework assignments so students have opportunities to ask questions and get help before taking the work home, and

- assignments for additional practice or peer tutoring or partner reading.

CREATING WORKSTATIONS TO EXTEND PRACTICE

Workstations are learning centers, that is, places where students gather and work on specific learning tasks. The activities completed in workstations are similar to the work teachers assign now, but students are allowed to complete the assignments collaboratively until sufficient instruction has occurred. Workstations provide excellent opportunities to extend instruction while you are working with another small group. By allowing students to work collaboratively and discuss or share their work at the workstations, the teaching and learning continues. When small groups of two or more students gather at a workstation to complete assignments, they are encouraged to provide constructive feedback and assistance to their peers. Using flexible and mixed skill groupings, students can help each other and extend instruction beyond the teaching table.

Some workstations can be single use only, such as a technology or computer station. Classrooms include single and multiple use workstations so students learn to work independently at a workstation or their desk and cooperatively in small groups at workstations, the worktable, and the teaching table. The number of workstations needed depends of the number of students who may be assigned to workstations during each small group period. Usually you need options for one-third to one-half of the class to choose or be assigned to workstations. If you are using three small group rotations, then you will need workstation opportunities to accommodate one-third of the students in your class, that is, approximately one-third of the students attends the teaching table while another third of the students completes written assignments or homework at the worktable, and the last third attends workstations. Table 4.1 describes this generic configuration.

When developing the workstations, you need to focus on usefulness and purpose for instruction, not artistic design. A workstation can be created by simply pushing several desks together to form a work area. A student assigned to be the Supply Monitor adds workbooks or worksheets, or whatever materials are needed

TABLE 4.1

24 STUDENTS IN CLASS		
TEACHING TABLE	WORKTABLE	WORKSTATIONS
1 table/space	1 table/space	2–4 centers
6–8 students	6–8 students	8–10 students, each attending workstations

to complete an assigned project. Students can complete work as a group or independently, depending on your directions for each activity or assignment, but everything in the center is to serve the main goal, which is practicing skills to become proficient learners.

You should not spend extraordinary amounts of time creating fancy workstations. Classroom environments using workstations can be created by rearranging the furniture and changing the way you allow students to work. Creating beautiful workstations is not the purpose. Your time should be focused on improving instructional delivery and effectiveness. Improving instruction and allowing you to spend more time with planning and thinking about effective ways to teach is more important than beautiful workstations.

Adjusting Mind-sets about Workstations

Some teachers have to adjust their mind-sets when using workstations. Students need to talk, share ideas, discuss findings, identify problems, and seek solutions. Learning needs to be proactive, not passive, and engaging so students remember what they do and say. Research on vocabularies and skills needed to be excellent readers has confirmed the need for students to verbalize their learning and practice using language in oral and written formats (Beck, McKeown, & Kucan, 2002; Carnine, Silbert, Kame'enui, & Tarver, 2004; Tyner, 2004; Vaughn & Linan-Thompson, 2004).

Students should be encouraged to actively participate in discussions using their words to communicate ideas, solve problems, and summarize results. Copying and sharing work are positive instructional elements because students practice skills correctly with the helpful guidance of a peer. Learning continues beyond teacher-led instruction. No longer is the quiet, submissive classroom considered the best model for instruction. Students are actively working in study groups to understand how to apply skills and increase knowledge. Teachers encourage students to work independently after they have observed their performance using a skill at the teaching table. Most students work independently once they feel confident in their skill set and seek assistance only when a question arises or they need clarification about something.

Adjusting How Workstations Are Used

Workstations are used differently in some classroom environments. Early childhood and kindergarten classrooms typically have learning centers or workstations that permit active participation with a stronger emphasis on social and personal development than academic skills. Workstations in these classes are often developed around themes that promote development of language and literacy, vocabulary, fine and gross motor skills for manipulation and discovery, and play activities. Activities usually do not require skills mastery and do not involve paper and pencil tasks. Students use manipulatives to discover and develop concepts while using personal and social skills for cooperative play or learning.

Elementary classroom workstations have a more academic focus, but they are used to complete activities involving workbook passages or assignments that provide practice with previously taught skills from the core reading program. Traditional instruction usually has students working independently on assigned seatwork, and students are not encouraged to work collaboratively. The problem with the traditional model is that some students need help or more frequent affirmation that they are doing something correctly. Therefore, they interrupt the teacher who is working with another small group or they ask another student, which is sometimes not allowed. Encouraging students to seek peer assistance prevents many interruptions for the teacher when he/she is working with another group.

Using workstations encourages students to share ideas and engage in discussions about a particular topic or assignment. They work and learn together to complete practice activities either as assigned partners or small group teams. Not every student needs to be completing the same assignment within a small group. Homework, reading, spelling, or writing assignments can vary, but students are allowed to seek help within their group as needed. Students can be assigned to read to each other, even if they are not reading from the same book. You can assign reading partners who can support each other and work together to practice reading text by following orchestrated roles that were taught previously (Mathes & Fuchs, 1994). Successful grouping will create opportunities for positive student interactions and support.

Assigning Different Activities at Workstations as Needed

Using different activities at workstations and the worktable and allowing students to complete different assignments represent a shift from traditional practice, but that is differentiating instruction. Students may not be completing the same activity when attending the worktable or some workstations. They may be completing activities that align to their core reading materials based on their reading level. Students will attempt to help each other anyway. Students will naturally peer tutor when allowed and assist as an interim teaching assistant when the classroom teacher is working with other students. Students provide explanations for their work that helps other students learn. While teachers are working with another small group, they hear and observe interactions at the workstations. That feedback is important for planning instruction and monitoring student progress. Students requesting more support or requiring more attention may need more instruction or the group membership may need to be changed.

Workstation activities are used for practice activities, not assessment, so sharing work and learning is encouraged. Depending on students' assignments, the activity to be completed, and the amount of prior instruction or practice, you decide whether students work in study groups or work alone at their desks for independent practice. Discussions help students verbalize their learning, cooperatively tutor others, understand concepts, and strengthen their skills through application. You create successful learning opportunities at the workstations by carefully grouping students to support within-group instruction and by selecting assignments that use skills that have been previously taught and practiced BEFORE students are expected to complete them with minimal teacher supervision or independently.

CHOOSING WORKSTATION ACTIVITIES

Sometimes teachers need to delay assigning some workstation activities or assignments until sufficient instruction has occurred. Assignments appearing in teacher editions in core reading programs introduce a specific skill in a reading lesson and offer practice activities to apply newly learned skills on the same day. Twenty minutes of reading instruction with the teacher is not sufficient instructional time to develop proficiency with a new skill and work without teacher guidance. It is an instructional error to assign independent work too soon, yet it frequently occurs in classrooms. Students attempt to complete the activity or assignment, but because they need help, they interrupt the teacher working with another group, or they misbehave.

Carefully choosing activities and assignments for workstations and the worktable creates successful learning experiences for students and prevents constant interruptions for teachers. Teaching students about accountability and responsibility is also helpful so that they realize that learning together supports them but they are still held accountable for their work and responsible for their growth academically and socially. Modeling expectations and teaching and training procedures enhance success:

- Model and teach your expectations for participating in workstation activities and role-play what-if situations so that students can add their input about potential solutions to problems.

- Provide sufficient modeling and instruction before assigning activities for worktable, homework, or workstations so that expectations for performance are clearly understood.

- Delay assigning activities that use new vocabulary or newly introduced concepts that require students to apply skills that have not been presented with sufficient modeling and instruction.

- Assign no task or activity as an independent activity until students demonstrate 70 percent mastery in a teacher-directed small group, including homework, seatwork, and activities at the worktable and workstations.

- Allow students to talk quietly, work collaboratively, and provide feedback to each other when completing practice assignments.

- Allow students to help each other edit and make corrections when the teacher is working with another group.

- Encourage students to check each other's work and ensure assignments are completed correctly and on time.

- Encourage students to work cooperatively and assist each other when cleaning up during transitions. Compliment efforts and achievements.

- Demonstrate how to ask for help when materials are needed for an activity in a workstation, that is, ask for assistance from the Supply Monitor, a student assigned to monitor use of supplies in classroom.

- Demonstrate how to ask for assistance from Workstation Monitors or Center Checkers, those assigned to monitor clean-up and use of workstation materials.

- Encourage students to request help from the Counselor, a student assigned to listen and help solve problems that may occur so the teacher is not interrupted while working with a small group.

VARYING THE USE OF WORKSTATIONS

Use workstations for a variety of activities. The types of workstations you use depend on the skills to be taught, the activities used to practice those skills, and students' interest. The following suggestions are commonly used classroom workstations.

- *Homework Station* Students are allowed to do homework assignments at school and receive assistance when needed before working independently at home to complete the assignment.

- *Language and Literacy Station* Students can read with an assigned partner or complete workbook pages from their reading program.

- *Vocabulary, Spelling, and Writing Station* Students participate in activities, games, or assignments that develop vocabulary word meanings and improve spelling and writing skills.

- *Special Projects and Creative Expression Station* Students use creative talents to develop projects or research artists and famous creations to complete written reports and share with classmates, thus integrating history, arts, and culture with reading, spelling, and writing instruction.

- *Author Study* Students are exposed to different books written by the same author to compare and contrast writing styles, illustrations, and different reading genres.

- *Technology Station* Students use computer-assisted practice activities to strengthen skills and provide additional guided practice.

- *Take Five* Students go here when they need a short break to calm down. A kitchen timer can be included so a student can take a 5 minute break and relax to recollect her/his thoughts, reflect on choices, and regroup her/his behavior before rejoining classmates. A headset and music may be provided.

Organizing Materials for Workstations

Math, science, and social studies may include manipulatives for discovery or investigation as well as books, paper, and writing utensils to integrate content and apply skills by reading to learn and writing to express ideas.

It is a good idea to organize materials for workstations in ways that promote successful teaching activities and group cooperation. The following suggestions should help you organize materials for workstations:

- Simplify transitions by using fewer activity choices per workstation. Students participate in workstations for 20 minutes or less during each small group period so they do not need multiple activity choices.

- Store all teaching materials in plastic containers with lids, organizing materials for specific themes, skills, or assignments. Use one container for each activity or assignment, that is, add writing materials such as paper, pencil, pen, crayons, and glue stick, or put each game or puzzle or activity in one plastic container with a lid.

- Organize plastic containers by theme or use, and label each by placing a sentence strip or index card on the ends that are visible when the containers are stacked. Stack the containers in a corner or in a storage area such as closet so that they are hidden from view and drape a cloth or sheet over the stack. Then materials appear new and interesting to students as they are used throughout the year.

- Stack plastic containers by use (month of year), or themes, or by skills so that they can be retrieved quickly.

- Change activities and assignments in workstations either weekly or biweekly simply by removing plastic containers and adding new ones.

- Place no more than three to four plastic containers in a workstation so cleanup can be completed on time. Two containers or choices are preferred so that students focus, get started with the activity, and are ready for cleanup within 20 minutes. Decide whether students are assigned to complete certain activities or if they can choose between activities at a particular workstation.

- Ensure that materials for each container are not similar in shape, color, or size so that students can easily sort materials into the appropriate containers when cleaning up, that is, puzzle or game pieces need to look distinctly different to facilitate placement in the correct containers and permit quick cleanup.

Labeling Workstations and Regulating Attendance

Label workstations and assign numbers that represent how many students can attend each workstation at one time. Regulating attendance prevents problems with too many students trying to share limited resources, that is, space, materials, or time. There are many ways to communicate the number of students allowed in a particular workstation at one time.

Some teachers post the name of the workstation by hanging a sign or poster from the ceiling, or they use a picture or label that is posted near the entry of each workstation. They may attach a numeral on that sign or label that indicates the workstation limit for student attendance. Numerals can be attached with magnets, clips, or sticky surfaces so they can be changed easily.

Some teachers prefer to use orange athletic cones with numerals printed on them to indicate student membership per workstation. You can cut numerals from construction paper and attach them to the athletic cones using clear adhesive tape. Students can quickly scan the classroom and locate the orange cones to determine which workstations have space available and are open for business. Cones are easily removed to close a workstation as needed. You then regulate students' choices by adding or removing cones from workstations. This procedure minimizes the time spent on discussion about what students want to do and can do. The cones help communicate choices for students at assigned times.

CHANGING HOW INSTRUCTION IS DELIVERED

Most teachers have a daily schedule that organizes instruction in larger blocks of time. Alternating time periods for whole class and small group instruction require teachers to divide instructional time into smaller parts. Daily schedules vary according to grade level assignments and the amount of time allocated for instruction. Some schedules also require adjustments to avoid conflicts with assigned activities such as recess, lunch, library, music, counseling, etc.

Teacher schedules can also vary. Teachers can be assigned instructional responsibilities for the full day, half day, or a few hours or minutes. Teachers with larger blocks of time in their schedule have more flexibility for change, and they can incorporate additional small group periods. Teacher assigned shorter periods for reading instruction usually must use larger group sizes in order to meet with each group every day.

Regardless of the amount of time you have for reading instruction each day, changing the daily schedule to alternate times for whole class and small group instruction creates order and predictability. A well-organized daily schedule posted in a classroom communicates expectations and reduces stress for teachers and students. Time management is needed to improve teacher and student outcomes.

Monitoring the Use of Instructional Time

Monitoring the use of instructional time is critical. Appendix E, Checklist for Monitoring Use of Instructional Time (C-MIT), provides a quick and easy way to help you monitor how instructional time is used. The checklist can be used to record observations while you are teaching. Usually the checklist is completed during a 20 minute walk-through observation. The chart helps teachers and coaches calculate how teachers use classroom time for behavioral, environmental, or instructional use.

Teaching students in small groups allows teachers to focus on explicit instruction targeted to individual needs. Teachers need help when developing daily schedules that include alternating periods for whole class and small group instruction. Different examples of daily schedules are provided below to illustrate how instructional time can be managed efficiently and incorporate flexible grouping patterns for differentiating instruction. These examples are included to demonstrate ways to alternate time periods for whole class and small group instruction for full day, partial day, 60 minute, or 90 minute reading blocks.

Use these formats as a guide to develop a daily schedule that works best for you and your students. First create a rough draft of your daily schedule and use it for a day or two. Marking notes on the draft copy helps you modify the schedule to create a best fit. Then make a final copy of the daily schedule and post it in your classroom. Daily schedules may change from day to day depending on other activities such as library, PE, or computer lab. Finally, be flexible enough to change it as needed.

In order to develop a daily schedule using whole class and small group instruction,

- Get a pen and a blank piece of lined paper.

- List the time that students enter your classroom on the first line.

- List the time that students leave your classroom on the last line.

- Estimate about mid-page and list the time the class goes to lunch (if applicable).

- Approximate and list times for prescheduled daily activities that cannot be changed, such as recess, physical education, or snack (if applicable).

- Use the margin to list other weekly events or activities such as library or music.

- Examine the framework created so far.

  - Locate blank spaces or periods that can be used for whole class and small group instruction.

  - Plan 15–20 minute periods for whole class lessons.

  - Plan 20–25 minutes for small group sessions, realizing that some groups may require less time, depending on skill or activity taught and the students' skills set within that group, that is, students working beyond level may not always need 20 minutes for small group.

  - Plan more time for transitions initially until students get used to the routines and procedures. As students become more proficient at making transitions, less time is required.

- Begin the day with a whole class activity using a graphic organizer as an overview to review previously taught skills and to provide clear directions for student performance that day.

- Mark time periods on the framework for alternating whole class and small groups. Count the number of time periods. Depending on the number of periods created for small groups, divide the names of students into that many groups. If there are three time periods for small groups, then divide students' names into three small groups.

- Alternate whole class and small group instruction if the schedule allows, or teach two small groups consecutively without a whole class time period between them.

- Schedule shorter periods of only 10–15 minutes between small groups for reading a story or partner reading. Remember that some of the whole class periods can be used for social studies or science activities if the content is used to teach reading skills. Teachers who have full day classes with the same students can integrate other subject area content and use it to apply previously taught reading skills. Remember that whole class instruction can be subdivided into smaller group practice opportunities by incorporating partnering.

- Post a copy of the daily schedule in classroom and make a copy for the substitute folder, administrator or supervisor, parents, and students.

Using Sample Daily Schedules to Help Organize Instructional Time

When examining sample daily schedules, you need to pay attention to the process, remembering the purpose of a sample is to demonstrate how instructional time can be used. The activities listed on the daily schedules below may or may not reflect the things that happen in your normal day. Use these sample schedules to personalize and create a schedule that will accommodate your needs and schedule demands.

HALF DAY

BASIC SCHEDULE
(3 HOURS OF INSTRUCTION/3 SMALL GROUPS)

8:00–8:25	Whole class overview
	Use graphic organizer to review important skills such as vocabulary words, model to demonstrate expectations, communicate expectations for the day.
8:25–8:30	Transition as students get ready to begin activities
	Assign students to help others get started.
	Teacher prepares to teach a small group lesson.
8:30–8:50	Small groups
	Teacher works with one group while other students work in preassigned activities such as small group assignments at a worktable or in workstations, or they complete independent work at desks.
8:50-9:00	Transition
	Teacher completes activity with small group and organizes materials for the next group. Students file papers and materials in designated places like mailbox or notebook, desk, or backpack. Students leave the teaching table and return to a designated place, that is, desk or carpet area to read books until the next activity begins or to complete assigned jobs.
9:00–9:15	Whole class activity
	Complete an activity from the lesson plans that is suitable for whole class, such as reading a story then creating a story web to review story structure or vocabulary.
9:15–9:20	Transition
9:20–9:40	Small groups
9:40–9:45	Transition
9:45–10:05	Whole class activity
10:05–10:25	Small groups
10:25–10:30	Transition
10:30–10:50	Whole class activity or partner reading
10:50–11:00	Wrap Up, final discussions, vocabulary review, review graphic organizer

MODIFICATION A

(3 HOUR SCHEDULE/3 SMALL GROUPS, 2 WHOLE CLASS ACTIVITIES, AND A BREAK FOR RECESS OR PE)

8:00–8:25	Whole class overview
8:25–8:30	Transition
8:30–8:50	Small groups
8:50–9:00	Transition
9:00–9:20	Small groups
9:20–9:25	Transition
9:25–9:45	Small groups
9:45–9:50	Transition
9:50–10:20	Recess or PE, library, or music
10:20–10:30	Transition
10:30–10:50	Whole class activity or partner reading
10:50–11:00	Whole class activity and Wrap Up

MODIFICATION B

(3 HOUR SCHEDULE/4 SMALL GROUPS, 2 WHOLE CLASS ACTIVITIES, AND A BREAK FOR PE)

8:00–8:25	Whole class overview
8:25–8:30	Transition
8:30–8:50	Small groups
8:50–9:00	Transition
9:00–9:20	Small groups
9:20–9:25	Transition
9:25–9:45	Small groups
9:45–10:05	Small groups
10:05–10:10	Transition
10:10–10:40	Recess or PE, library, or music
10:40–10:50	Transition
10:50–11:00	Whole class activity and Wrap Up

MODIFICATION C

(3 HOUR SCHEDULE/4 GROUPS, 3 WHOLE CLASS ACTIVITIES, AND A BREAK FOR PE)

8:00–8:25	Whole class overview
8:25–8:30	Transition
8:30–8:50	Small groups
8:50–9:00	Transition
9:00–9:20	Small groups
9:15–9:30	Whole class
9:30–9:35	Transition
9:35–9:55	Small groups
9:55–10:00	Transition
10:00–10:20	Recess or PE, library, or music

10:20–10:30	Transition
10:30–10:50	Small groups
10:50–11:00	Whole class activity and Wrap Up

DAILY SCHEDULE FOR 60 MINUTES OF READING INSTRUCTION

(2 SMALL GROUPS/90 MINUTES OR 1.5 HOURS)

8:00–8:15	Whole class overview using graphic organizer
8:15–8:20	Transition
8:20–8:40	Small groups
8:40–9:10	Small groups
9:10–9:15	Transition
9:15–9:30	Whole class activity and Wrap Up

DAILY SCHEDULE FOR 90 MINUTES OF READING INSTRUCTION

(3 SMALL GROUPS/90 MINUTES OR 1.5 HOURS)

8:00–8:10	Whole class overview using graphic organizer
8:10–8:15	Transition
8:15–8:35	Small groups
8:35–8:40	Transition
8:40–9:00	Small groups
9:00–9:05	Transition
9:05–9:25	Small groups
9:25–9:30	Whole class activity and Wrap Up

DAILY SCHEDULE FOR 2 HOURS OF READING INSTRUCTION

(4 SMALL GROUPS/120 MINUTES OR 2 HOURS)

8:00–8:10	Whole class overview using graphic organizer
8:10–8:15	Transition
8:15–8:35	Small groups
8:35–8:40	Transition
8:40–9:00	Small groups
9:00–9:05	Transition
9:05–9:25	Small groups
9:25–9:30	Transition
9:30–9:50	Small groups
9:50–10:00	Whole class activity and Wrap Up

FULL DAY SCHEDULE

(WHOLE CLASS AND SMALL GROUP INSTRUCTION/GROUPING ALL DAY)

8:00–8:10	Whole class overview using graphic organizer
8:10–8:15	Transition
8:15–8:35	Small groups
8:35–8:40	Transition
8:40–9:00	Small groups
9:00–9:05	Transition
9:05–9:25	Small groups
9:25–9:30	Transition
9:30–9:50	Small groups
9:50–10:00	Whole class activity for spelling, writing
10:00–10:15	Reading break, read with partners or independently to relax
10:15–10:40	Whole class activity
10:45–11:00	Peer-assisted group work to complete assignment related to whole class activity at 10:15–10:40
10:40–11:00	Check work and file in mailboxes, students complete work in Do/Done Folder
11:00–11:30	Whole class activity, math
11:30–12:00	Lunch
12:00–12:30	Recess, break, library, or computer lab
12:30–12:50	Small groups, math
12:55–1:25	Small groups, math
1:30–2:00	Whole class activity, social studies or science
2:00–2:25	Small groups, math
2:25–2:45	Whole class activity
2:45–3:00 or later	Whole class activity and Wrap Up using graphic organizer

Extending Grouping to All Day or Modifying Schedules for Special Events

Many teachers extend using small and whole group instruction all day. Reading and language arts activities are used in the morning with cross-curricular activities from science and social studies used to apply reading and writing skills. Small group instruction in the afternoon focuses on math and science skills that are explicitly taught at the teaching table. You may want to incorporate the following suggestions into your instructional day:

- Create a daily schedule that includes rotations using whole class and small group instruction all day. Teach other academic subjects at the teaching table, teaching math or reading texts for science or social studies while incorporating reading instruction.

- Switch times for whole class and small groups to best fit events that day, that is, if library, PE, or music classes are scheduled on a particular day, then omit one of the whole class sessions. Use flexible pacing to adjust to needs.

- Alternate whole class and small group activities if preferred and time permits.

- Teach all small groups before trying to get another whole class wrap up activity completed and review later in the day if possible.

- Ensure all students meet and work in a small group for teacher-directed, data-informed instruction every day if possible.

- Plan at least one to two times a month to allow time for you to listen as each student reads aloud so fluency and complete error analysis can be monitored to determine what skills may need reteaching or reviewing.

MONITORING INSTRUCTIONAL PACING

Use a kitchen timer to maintain a perky instructional pace and stay on schedule. Assign a student to be Timekeeper to help monitor use of instructional time. It's best to purchase a kitchen timer that ends with zero seconds remaining at the top and attach colored adhesive paper dots or use a permanent marker to create visuals on the timer to assist students who do not know how to tell time. The colored dots indicate when instruction begins, when transitions are about to happen, and when an activity ends (See Figure 4.4).

- Put a green dot by the numeral 20 to indicate the start position for 20 minute small group periods.

- Put a yellow dot by the numeral 5 to indicate 5 minutes until a transition or change occurs.

FIGURE 4.4
Kitchen timer used to monitor instructional pacing.

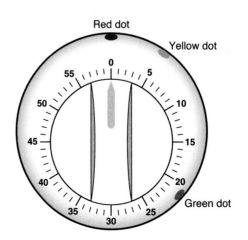

- Put a red dot by the zero to indicate time to stop and make a transition or change in activity.

- Set the time at the beginning of each small group activity to help with pacing. Have the Timekeeper monitor the clock. Set the clock out of reach for younger students so they are not tempted to "help" the clock keep time.

- Have the assigned student (or Timekeeper) move quietly through the room when the timer reaches the yellow dot indicating 5 minutes until a transition and say, "Five minutes until we change." The Timekeeper has permission to leave any area to provide the warning before a transition occurs.

- Use the 5 minute warning at the teaching table to indicate a shift in instruction. Stop teaching and begin asking questions to assess if students understood instruction or need a reteach the following day, or just review and wrap up the lesson. Students should summarize the lesson to a partner while you listen to determine their needs. Chart observations on mailing labels as you listen to students.

Encourage students to use transitions for personal needs: bathroom breaks, getting a drink, organizing supplies, checking their Do/Done Folder, or filing papers in their mailbox. Students can chat quietly with peers during transitions or consult with you for assistance.

CHAPTER SUMMARY

Sharing responsibilities in the classroom community helps teachers and students work cooperatively and collaboratively to ensure success. Students can serve as classroom helpers or teaching assistants by sharing the workload for environmental management or instruction. When students assist with responsibilities in the classroom, teachers spend more time teaching.

Teachers use a daily schedule that alternates time periods for whole class and small group instruction. They develop a job chart to delegate responsibilities to students and create more time for them to teach. Assigned jobs are completed before and after class and during transitions from whole class and small group activities. A daily schedule and job chart helps organize instructional delivery so more time is spent on teaching and learning.

RESOURCES THAT HELP

www.eduplace.com/rdg/res/classroom.html
Provides basic ideas and procedures for setting up the classroom for instructional success.

www.mspowell.com/otherwebpages/transitiontips.htm
Provides ideas for setting children up for success when transitioning between workstations or daily routines in the classroom.

www.readingrockets.org/articles/c93
Provides articles detailing preventative approaches to classroom management and classroom arrangement.

www.garlicpress.com
Provides American Sign Language materials, including hand signs, that may be used to communicate expectations such as "Five minutes," "Stop," "Go," or "Make a choice now please." Also provides materials for vocabulary and reading instruction for workstations, worktables, and teaching tables.

CHAPTER 5

Rotation Charts and Flexible Grouping

TEACHERS CAN USE ROTATION CHARTS TO VISUALLY REINFORCE ROUTINES that create structure and security in their classrooms. These charts help students know what to expect, how to organize and plan their day, what they will do, and with whom they will do it. This knowledge both empowers and assures. The students are not kept in the dark; instead they feel a sense of understanding and ownership toward the learning schedules. They are reassured, knowing that eventually they will work with the teacher and collaborate at the worktable and in the workstations with their peers.

Rotation charts communicate expectations and maintain order in the classroom environment. Creating a system for getting through the day or period of instruction helps students focus on what needs to be done. Structure is provided that communicates how and when things will be done. Students learn systematic procedures for participating in activities that include student decision making. Rotation charts provide a visual road map for student participation in activities that have been selected by the teacher after reviewing student data to determine what instruction is needed. Lists of students' names can be used with the chart to indicate group memberships. Students learn to locate their name on a list that shows small group membership and quickly determine where and with whom they will work at the teaching table, worktable, or the workstations. Rotation charts help student learn to apply organizational planning by reducing the confusion, arguments, or discussions about what happens next.

A rotation chart clearly depicts activity choices and group memberships. It illustrates when a student will participate and what group they will work with, and it guarantees opportunities for teacher attention at a teaching table. The rotation chart allows teachers to use similar skill and mixed skill groupings to develop relationships and support systems using peers.

CREATING ROUTINES AND PROCEDURES WITH A ROTATION CHART

Use a rotation chart to communicate expectations and maintain control of the classroom environment. Students learn to follow systematic procedures for participating in activities. Rotation charts:

- clearly and visually depict a road map for student movement,

- quietly and visually communicate expectations in a busy classroom,

- help stabilize and control choice and activities in the environment,

- allow students to make choices and learn decision making,

- create daily structure and promote consistency in routines,

- minimize time wasted during transitions,

- maximize use of instructional time,

- provide opportunities for whole class and small group explicit instruction,

- establish a system for differentiation through flexible grouping, and

- provide for behavior management by carefully selecting group memberships.

DEVELOPING A ROTATION CHART

Many kinds of rotation charts can be used to direct the movements of several small groups. These charts can be easily created with inexpensive and accessible supplies. Depending on resources and need, a variety of materials can be used to create a chart: construction paper, poster board, magnet boards, bulletin boards, or pocket charts. For example, a poster board can be used to construct the chart, and notepaper can be used to list names of students assigned to each group. The lists of names can be attached with sticky materials, magnets, pushpins, or metal clips.

Figure 5.1 shows a rotation chart that includes four activities at the bottom of the chart: teaching table, two workstations, and a worktable. Lists of student names are attached at the top to identify group membership. The number of students assigned to each group varies according to student needs for skills-focused instruction. The lists are attached with an adhesive or sticky material that allows easy removal when teachers use different grouping patterns for specific activities.

HELPING STUDENTS IDENTIFY GROUP ASSIGNMENTS

Different methods may be used to help students remember their group assignment. During the first two weeks, it is best to make minimal changes in the group memberships. Change memberships if it is necessary to create compatible groupings. Try not change memberships until students have established routines and clearly understand expectations. Flexible groupings may be used later when students have more experiences with the routines.

You may want to color code the names of your groups red, blue, yellow, and green. After assigning group names as colors, try using one of the following techniques to help younger students remember their group assignment:

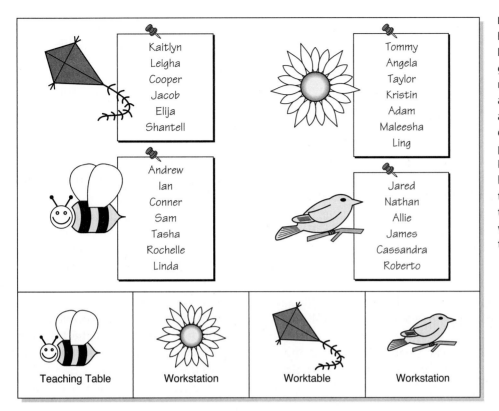

FIGURE 5.1
Rotation Chart Using Four Activities Student group names and memberships are shown at the top. Group names are rotated clockwise to designate how groups participate in activitites. Example: Sunflowers begin at workstation, then go to worktable, then to another workstation, and finally to the teaching table.

- Purchase rolls of plastic surveyor's tape, which comes in bright colors, from a local hardware store. Cut the tape into 8-inch strips. Tie one strip on each student's wrist, matching the tape color to the group membership color, that is, tie a yellow tape on the wrist of a student assigned to the yellow group. Because the tape is a lightweight plastic, it stretches easily and is comfortable.

- Paint one or more fingernails on a student's hand using the same color polish as the group membership color. A student assigned to red group, for example, might have red fingernail polish on the thumb of the left hand.

- Have the students wear colored necklaces or badges that indicate what groups they are assigned to.

MODELING HOW TO READ A ROTATION CHART

Assign a student to be the Chart Caller. You model how to read the chart and guide students to activities. Use explicit instructions for following the rotation chart, "If you are in the yellow group, please stand up. Yellow group, go to the teaching table." Then the teacher proceeds to name each student assigned to the yellow group. Once students know what group they "travel" with, it is not necessary to have students stand up as a group before sending them to the teaching table. Later, it will not be necessary to say students' names either. Just call the group name and identify where they are to go when it is time for them to go to a workstation. The Chart Caller will announce, "Yellow group, go to the teaching table now please," and the students in the yellow group will get up and go there. At first this process takes some time, but soon the transitions from activity to activity become familiar. Following the same routines is critical when reading the rotation chart. First, teachers model how to "read" the chart and guide students to activities beginning with the first activity on the left, the teaching table. Later, a Chart Caller assumes this role.

Groups rotate through activities (an important skill in itself) to ensure that all students participate, that is, after students attend the teaching table, other groups of students are directed to workstations or a worktable. Once the routines are established, the student Chart Caller directs students to activities while the teacher begins instruction at the teaching table. The Chart Caller begins the process by calling groups to the teaching table and worktable because these are usually seated activities and students can begin the work once the teacher arrives at the teaching table. In Figure 5.1, the Bumblebees would go to the teaching table. The Chart Caller would announce, "Bumblebees, go to the teaching table now please." Then the Kites would be directed to the worktable. The Chart Caller would say, "Kites, go to the teaching table now please." Then, the Chart Caller would announce, "Sunflowers, go to X workstation," if the teacher is directing the flow of activities and chooses which workstations the students will attend for a given period. (Later, when routines and procedures are established, students can be allowed to choose a workstation.) Last, the Redbirds would be directed to an assigned workstation or would pick one. After the Chart Caller has directed all students to their work areas, he/she joins his/her group for instruction.

Remember that consistency is critical for students to develop school behaviors that include routines and procedures for getting through the day. In the beginning, just getting students to go to a particular area and remain there is a huge accomplishment. Follow these suggestions for reading and implementing the rotation chart consistently:

- Use the same language for directions, "Go to the teaching table now please."

- Use consistent procedures for guiding students to activities, for example, send the groups to the teaching table, then worktable, then workstations.

- Model expectations with consistency until routines are learned.

- Provide encouraging feedback as students develop habits.

- Follow through always, that is, use the 3 Cs: Be *clear* explaining expectations, be *consistent* with follow through, and *complete* tasks.

- Clarify group memberships if students cannot read names on lists. Use a system to identify students in each membership, as noted above.

There is a purposeful and preferred order for using a rotation chart. First send students to small group work areas, the teaching table where they will participate in teacher-led small group differentiated skills instruction, and the worktable. About half of the students are now seated either at the teaching table and worktable. The remaining students are waiting to attend a workstation. They are thinking about their decision about where they will work, if choices are allowed. Then, the Chart Caller guides students to assigned workstations by calling on the group assigned to attend to workstations after leaving the teaching table. When routines are established, students can be allowed to choose the order in which they complete activities at the workstations. Rotating students through workstation activities ensures that everyone participates in all activities at some point during each day or week.

SETTING ROUTINES FOR GROUP PARTICIPATION

A number of things happen simultaneously at the beginning of a small group session while the Chart Caller is directing students to activities:

- The teacher sets the timer for 20 minutes and begins small group instruction at the teaching table.

- Students begin working at the worktable (often used for homework assignments).

- If needed, a counselor may be working with another student.

- The Supply Monitor may be loaning or checking out materials to students who cannot find their pencil, pen, paper, etc. This is usually completed during the transition between activities, prior to working in a workstation.

- The Timekeeper watches the timer so she/he can provide a 5 minute warning before the small group time period ends and a transition occurs.

- The Chart Caller joins his/her group once all students are participating in activities.

Allow Choices after Routines Are Established

Students assigned to or choosing a workstation are held accountable for their assignment or choice. Therefore, they are not allowed to change their minds and change workstations once the activity has started and the Chart Caller has determined all students are in the appropriate places for that instructional period. The purpose of not allowing students to change is clear. Students are encouraged to accept responsibilities for assigned work and realize the importance of accepting the authority of the decision leader, that is, teacher. Further, when students are allowed to choose workstations, they learn to consider all of their options and make a good choice. This helps students learn to be accountable and responsible for their decision making and develop an understanding that outcomes or consequences are directly linked to their choices. Students learn to think about their options and choose carefully because they are not allowed to make a second choice.

Allowing students to choose workstations has many advantages, and it can be used on some days but not all. You can plan activities for the workstations that cover instructional content and purpose for the day, for several days, or a week. If the activities are planned to be completed daily and a rotation chart is in use, then the students will have a choice of two workstations. If you use several workstations with activities to be completed by the end of the week, students have more choices and can use a contract to monitor which activities still need to be completed. You should limit the number of students that can work in each workstation. Activities and assignments at the workstations are planned to be completed within a 20 minute period, or you can have students return to the workstation and work on the same project for several days.

When choosing workstations, the group following the teaching table will choose first. The group following the worktable will choose last. This is helpful for teaching students to think about choices, make a good decision, and be prepared to accept the fact that the workstation they wanted to attend is full. Students must make another choice and have a "plan B," a second choice. If the students choosing the first time select a particular workstation, then students choosing in the second group have to select some other workstation. It is interesting to see this impact on some students. They have to be flexible in their decision making and acceptable in their responses when they do not get to participate according to their first choice. This is a teachable moment in itself for self-regulation and tolerance when students learn to compliantly accept second choices.

When students are allowed to make choices for workstations, more flexible groupings are used because students select whom to work with. But because of the restrictions on the number of students who can attend a workstation and how the two groups choose workstations, some students may work with students not assigned to their group. This occurs when students are assigned to four groups and there are two groups choosing workstations during that small group instructional period. However, when students are allowed to choose workstations, you may find that a few students are not able to work collaboratively in a workstation and share their work until sufficient instruction has occurred. If that happens, regroup the students or assign workstations, disallowing choices. You can then ensure that less cooperative students with limited tolerance for others never choose the same workstations.

Adjust the Rotation Chart to Reflect Activity Changes

When a period for small group instruction ends, it is time to move to the next activity, that is, make a rotation. The Chart Caller returns to the rotation chart and moves the pictures of the group names at the bottom of the chart to reassign groups to activities. First, the Chart Caller removes the picture on the far right box at the bottom of the chart and lays it down. Next, the Chart Caller rotates the pictures clockwise moving each one to the right. Last, the Chart Caller picks up the picture that was removed first and places it in the box for the teaching table. After each small group time, the Chart Caller follows this procedure to change the chart and reassign student groups to activities.

Rotation charts help teachers provide clear, consistent, and complete directions for getting through the day. The chart clearly identifies what the rest of the students are doing when the teacher is working with a small group. Some advantages of using rotation charts for behavioral and environmental management include:

- Encourages consistency with routines for participation and behavior
- Develops student responsibility and accountability for participating, peer tutoring, and making quick transitions
- Helps students self-regulate and follow routines to complete tasks
- Proactively creates behavioral compliance using grouping to separate students who may not need to work together
- Encourages students to make good choices because they will be held accountable for that choice
- Teaches students to consider all options carefully before making a choice of a workstation so they learn accountability and responsibility for their decision making and understand that outcomes, or consequences, are directly related to their choice

USING A ROTATION CHART FOR FLEXIBLE GROUPING

Teachers use flexible groupings to engage students collaboratively and to differentiate instruction for practice activities. Small groups include mixed skill-set groupings to encourage peer tutoring with constructive feedback when the teacher is working with other students. In order to develop flexible grouping,

- use data to create homogeneous or similar skill-set groupings. Print students' names on blue paper to create the lists for the chart.
- use data to create heterogeneous or mixed skill-set groupings. Print students' names on yellow paper to create the lists for the chart.
- use grouping within grouping patterns. Use data to create partners, or smaller groups within the small groups, that is, assign 6 students to a small group and create three sets of reading partners. Print students' names on light green paper to create the lists for the chart. This is shown in Figure 5.2.

FIGURE 5.2
Grouping Patterns

Homogeneous Groups
Student names appear on blue paper indicating to the teacher
that students have been assigned to small groups homogeneously.

Group 1	Group 2	Group 3
Chris	Evangelina	Ernesto
Jenny	Marcus	Weston
Tim	Tamoko	Heidi
Estavan	Teresa	Franchesca
Ramon	Sarah	Renaldo
Lisa	Juan	Stephanie
Colleen	Nader	Niko
Manuel	Ian	Julie
Ellie	Eita	Laurie
Kahn		

Heterogeneous Groups
Student names appear on yellow paper indicating to the teacher
that students have been assigned to small groups heterogeneously.

Group 1	Group 2	Group 3
Chris	Jenny	Sarah
Evangelina	Marcus	Weston
Tim	Lisa	Heidi
Estavan	Franchesca	Teresa
Ramon	Ernesto	Renaldo
Tamoko	Juan	Stephanie
Colleen	Nader	Niko
Manuel	Kahn	Julie
Ellie	Eita	Laurie
Ian		

Partners for Mixed or Flexible Groups
Student names appear on green paper indicating to the teacher
that students have been assigned as partners within a small group.

Group 1	Group 2	Group 3
Chris + Evangelina	Marcus + Lisa	Ernesto + Julie
Jenny + Ian	Tamoko + Ramon	Franchesca + Ellie
Tim + Sarah	Colleen + Juan	Renaldo + Eita
Estavan + Teresa	Nader + Stephanie	Kahn + Laurie
	Manuel + Heidi	Niko + Julie

Select the grouping pattern that works best for teaching the needed skills and for differentiating instruction. If the skill to be practiced can be taught or practiced using mixed skill groupings, then you use the group memberships listed on yellow paper. If you are introducing a new skill or evaluating student achievement, you can use the group memberships listed on blue paper. Then instruction at the teaching table will be conducted with similar skill groupings. You simply exchange the group membership lists or reassign students to group memberships to incorporate flexible grouping. Students learn to locate their name on the group membership lists on the rotation chart and follow the order of activities as indicated by the chart.

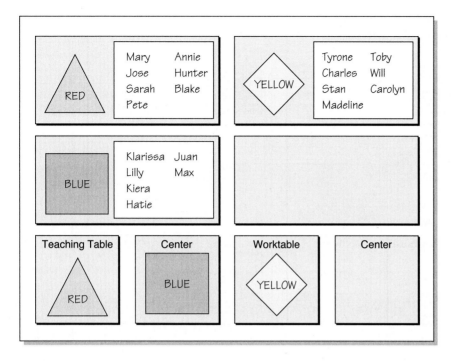

FIGURE 5.3
Rectangular chart using
3 small groups

Modify the Rotation Chart to Respond to Needs

Teachers can modify the rotation chart according to their needs. The chart can be used to direct two to four small groups through two to four activities. Examine the data and determine needs for instruction, then group students for instruction. After creating a daily schedule and determining how many small group time periods can be used, you can determine how to use the rotation chart and guide students through activities.

Modification A using 3 groups and 3 Activity Choices (teaching table, the worktable and one workstation or center)   The pictures at the bottom of the chart are rotated in a clockwise procedure from left to right to guide students through activities the same as before. This rotation works best when total instructional time is 90–120 minutes (See Figure 5.3).

Modification B using 2 Groups and 2 Activity Choices (the Teaching Table and the Worktable)   This rotation works best when total instructional time is 60–90 minutes (See Figure 5.4).

It is strongly recommended that schools implementing the management system in all grade levels use the rectangular chart with four rotation options at the bottom of the chart: a teaching table, a worktable, and two workstations. It provides more consistency in routines and procedures for students and allows more flexibility for teachers to modify its use with two to four student groups. Some teachers prefer to use a circular rotation chart that is designed to subdivide the whole class in three smaller groups.

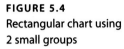

FIGURE 5.4
Rectangular chart using
2 small groups

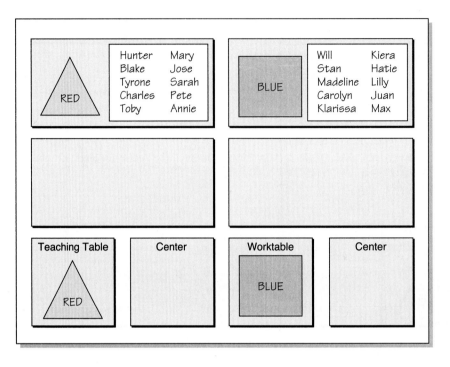

USING A CIRCULAR ROTATION CHART TO GUIDE STUDENTS

A circular rotation chart may be used to rotate small groups through instructional activities at a teaching table, a worktable, and a workstation. Lists that identify small group memberships are posted on the bulletin board by the rotation chart. Student groups rotate clockwise through activities as before. Teacher-directed instruction occurs at the teaching table. Students can complete written assignments or projects at the workstations and worktable. Some teachers allow students to begin their homework at the worktable so help is available if needed.

Teachers with only 50–60 minute class periods may need this configuration. Teacher-led instruction occurs with approximately one-half of the students for 20 minutes, then the other half of the class for 20 minutes. When not working with the teacher, students can work at either a workstation or a worktable. Using student contracts, students complete the work at the worktable and workstations during the week.

Using the format in Figure 5.5, students can choose to attend either the worktable or workstations. Teachers may alternate days for small groups. They use this format, allowing students to choose activities on Monday, Wednesday, and Friday and on Tuesday and Thursday. Students attend workstations on some days and the worktable on the next day. Allowing students to make choices is recommended after the routines have been established. You must carefully select which group memberships can choose activities for workstations at the same time. Some students who do not work well together may choose the same activity using this format.

You may choose to use a different configuration for 90–120 minute instructional periods. Students are divided into three groups that attend each activity for 20–25 minutes, as in Figure 5.6.

Two Small Groups: 50–60 Minute Block
Students work in small groups at worktable or independently at desk.

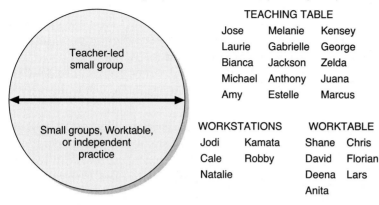

TEACHING TABLE

Jose	Melanie	Kensey
Laurie	Gabrielle	George
Bianca	Jackson	Zelda
Michael	Anthony	Juana
Amy	Estelle	Marcus

WORKSTATIONS

Jodi	Kamata
Cale	Robby
Natalie	

WORKTABLE

Shane	Chris
David	Florian
Deena	Lars
Anita	

FIGURE 5.5
Circular Chart Using Two
Time Periods or Groups

Three Small Groups: 90 Minute Block
Students may work in small study groups at worktable or independently at desk.

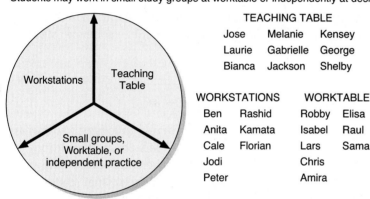

TEACHING TABLE

Jose	Melanie	Kensey
Laurie	Gabrielle	George
Bianca	Jackson	Shelby

WORKSTATIONS

Ben	Rashid
Anita	Kamata
Cale	Florian
Jodi	
Peter	

WORKTABLE

Robby	Elisa
Isabel	Raul
Lars	Samara
Chris	
Amira	

FIGURE 5.6
Circular Chart Using
Three Small Groups

Four Small Groups: 90–120 Minute Block

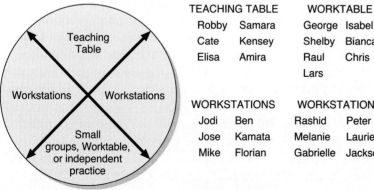

TEACHING TABLE

Robby	Samara
Cate	Kensey
Elisa	Amira

WORKTABLE

George	Isabel
Shelby	Bianca
Raul	Chris
Lars	

WORKSTATIONS

Jodi	Ben
Jose	Kamata
Mike	Florian

WORKSTATIONS

Rashid	Peter
Melanie	Laurie
Gabrielle	Jackson

FIGURE 5.7
Circular Chart Using Four
Small Groups

Teachers use the circular chart shown in Figure 5.7 when using three to four small group sessions during a 90–120 minute instructional period. Students can be divided into three to four small groups. Each group attends an activity for 20–25 minutes.

ENCOURAGING STUDENT DECISION MAKING AND TUTORING

You decide which choices are available and allow students to make decisions within those boundaries. In the beginning, students learn the routines and procedures much quicker when no choice of workstations is allowed. Once consistency is maintained, then implement flexible groupings. To begin, you decide what activities and materials will be used and what student groupings will work best for those activities.

Students may need coaching to help with decision making and choosing activities at the workstations. Students, regardless of small group placement, can participate at some workstations and work together, that is, partners can read to each other from different books and help each other complete written assignments that vary in level of difficulty or skills application. Students can be taught how to peer tutor. Tutoring extends the learning to other small group activities when the teacher is working with one small group. Providing extra practice repetitions with more modeling dramatically increases skill levels. Students benefit when they tutor because it makes them process and use the information in a different way, thus students serving as tutors benefit from the experience (Mathes & Fuchs, 1994).

Establish Routines for Transitions

Maintaining a perky pace for instruction and consistently following routines and procedures helps reduce time spent on transitions. Teachers create routines and procedures for making smooth transitions quickly. There are several things you can do to demonstrate and verbalize clear expectations about what students may or may not do. Assign students to serve as assistants and to help facilitate smooth transitions and get students ready for the next activity. Encourage student assistants to help their classmates who have not completed their work at a workstation so you can continue instruction without interruption. Valuable time is saved when teachers begin instruction without waiting until everything and everyone is ready. Send student assistants such as the Counselor or a Workstation Monitor to help students who are not ready to move on. You will find that students often respond better and quicker when their peers request their assistance. There is usually less negative feedback or noncompliant behavior when a peer provides assistance.

Students with assigned jobs will be moving about the classroom during transitions to check on their responsibilities. Those without assigned jobs can read independently or with a friend, work on homework at their desk, or simply rest until the next activity begins. Some teachers play music or set a timer during transitions to indicate change is in progress. When the music or timer stops, that is the signal for beginning a new activity.

During transitions, you are finalizing the lesson with the small group and organizing materials for next group coming to the teaching table. The Timekeeper is monitoring the overall progress of cleanup during transitions. The Mailbox

Monitor is assisting with paper management, if needed. The Counselor, Supply Monitor, Workstation Monitors/Center Checkers, and the Trash or Environmental Monitor are moving around the classroom, complimenting their peers for their efforts and participation, and supervising and assisting as needed to reorganize and prepare for the next activity. Once routines are established, transitions become quick and easy and few undesirable behaviors occur. While some teachers have achieved seamless and smooth transitions in only two full days of instruction, most require more time with a good deal of coaching and support before efficient transitions become a reality.

Use Student Contracts

Some teachers use student contracts to communicate expectations for a week's performance. Contracts help students plan and use their time wisely to complete assignments. There are many advantages to using contracts:

- Students learn to pace themselves and create rough drafts of written assignments. They learn to work toward a goal or completed project whose activities or assignments have completion due dates at the end of a week or two weeks, or even a month for special projects.

- Students practice organizational planning and learn to monitor their performance and progress or achievement.

- Expectations for task completion are clearly communicated to other professionals working with students and to parents or guardians.

- Completed contracts can be attached to documents such as report cards or evaluation reports.

Student contracts can be used with both young children and older students. Use fewer words and more pictures to communicate expectations for younger students. Teachers should review contracts frequently to model how to use written criteria to organize, monitor, and evaluate performance. Contracts are filed in the mailboxes or Do/Done Folders until sent home. When students complete activities at a worktable or workstation early, they can review their contract and determine what to do next. You can check the mailboxes and review the student contracts to monitor students' pacing and practice or to chart personalized notes on the contract.

CHAPTER SUMMARY

Productive students have places to go, people to see, and things to do. Rotation charts help teachers and students maintain a productive and academically profitable schedule. These charts communicate daily structure by identifying small group memberships and activity choices. Rotation charts become a road map for classroom participation by illustrating the order in which students participate in activities. Teachers select how many groups to use and manipulate group names on the chart to design how small groups will be managed to incorporate flexible grouping. Grouping patterns and group memberships vary according to the skills taught or type of practice activities. Rotation charts allow teachers to direct the activities in the classroom, pace instruction, and control how students will participate so everyone is successful.

RESOURCES THAT HELP

www.nifl.gov/partnershipforreading/publications/reading_first1.html
Summarizes the findings of the National Reading Panel Report on successfully teaching children to read. Analysis and discussion are provided in phonemic awareness, phonics, fluency, vocabulary, and text comprehension.

www.nifl.gov/partnershipforreading/questions/questions_about.html
Provides a question-and-answer format to frequently asked questions about reading instruction.

www.readingrockets.org/teaching/reading101
Gives information on how children learn and the components of effective reading instruction.

www.texasreading.org/utcrla/materials/primary_word_analysis.asp
Provides insight into word analysis and its importance to reading success, activities for teaching word analysis, and approaches to monitoring children's progress in word recognition.

www.ed.gov/teachers/landing.jhtml?src=pn
Provides quick and easy access to thousands of educational resources found on various federal, state, university, nonprofit, and commercial Internet sites that can be used in creating lesson plans for the classroom.

www.teach-nology.com/tutorials/teaching/differentiate/planning/
Gives numerous tools and resources to supplement planning for curriculum and daily classroom activities.

www.teach-nology.com
Provides a wide variety of teacher resources, including lesson planning, rubrics, and Web sites.

www.nea.org/reviews/freebkstations05.html
This site from the National Education Association offers guidance on establishing routines for independent reading and response writing, as well as step-by-step instructions on how to set up and manage a variety of hands-on literacy workstations appropriate for students in grades 3 through 6.

www.ascd.org/portal/site/ascd/menuitem.4247f922ca8c9ecc8c2a9410d3108a0c/
An online dictionary, A Lexicon of Learning, that uses everyday words to define educational terms.

http://readwritethink.org/literacy/index.html
Provides methods for teachers to engage students in daily literacy activities to learn language (as students listen to it and use it with others in their everyday lives), learn about language (as students try to figure out how it works), and learn through language (as students use it to learn about or do something).

www.stenhouse.com
Provides articles comparing traditional learning centers and literacy workstations and also ideas for literacy workstations for reading instruction.

www.canteach.ca/elementary/beginning10.html
Provides examples of ideas for literacy workstations appropriate for students in grades kindergarten through second grade.

http://teachingheart.net/LC.htm
www.geocities.com/jankwv/centertime.html
Provide a look into classrooms that teach using workstations. Classroom management, work station ideas, and pictures are included.

http://teachers.net/lessons/posts/2399.html
Provides literacy workstation ideas for second semester kindergarten students.

www.ade.state.az.us/AZReads/reading1st

www.uth.tmc.edu/circle/best_practices.htm
Provides visual examples of classroom management options.

CHAPTER 6

Coaching for Success

T EACHERS NEED SUPPORT FROM A COLLEAGUE TO MAKE THE CHANGES necessary for implementing the suggestions presented in this book. This chapter defines and describes the important role that coaching can play in providing support for differentiating instruction in classrooms. It also provides some specific suggestions on how colleagues can successfully collaborate for student success.

COACHING IS NEEDED FOR DIFFERENTIATED INSTRUCTION

In Chapter 1 we noted, "Teachers often rely on personal educational experiences as their model for good instruction; they teach the way they learned." Implementing the ideas presented in the previous chapters of this book requires many—if not most—teachers to rethink and redesign their classrooms in fundamental and profound ways. These kinds of major changes can be nearly impossible to make, even when there is a high degree of willingness and excitement on the part of teachers.

In large part this difficulty is due to the fact that teachers are busy—every day—with the immediate and often challenging demands of teaching their students and managing their classrooms as they are currently configured. Shifting the way they teach simply takes an enormous effort. Teachers will need much more than a just a good idea, a plan, and motivation to create a classroom environment in which they can effectively implement differentiated instruction. Teachers who undertake the challenge of restructuring their classrooms to implement this new instruction will benefit from coaching support.

COACHING

Coaching is a way to support teachers in their efforts to provide high-quality instruction in academic areas, including reading, math, and science. Coaching is quickly becoming a popular model in schools for providing job-embedded, individualized, and sustained professional development to teachers (Annenberg Institute for School Reform, 2004; Bean, Swan, & Knaub, 2003).

Depending on how their role is structured and defined, academic or instructional coaches engage in a variety of school activities. These activities may include observing lessons and providing feedback to teachers, modeling effective teaching techniques and strategies, advising and supporting teachers to improve lesson design and implementation (materials, planning, instruction, and assessments), fostering team teaching, conducting workshops to introduce teachers to new strategies, helping teachers with classroom organization and management, developing and monitoring school improvement plans and goals, and designing systemic and structural changes, including class schedules, team meetings, school calendar, etc., to improve student academic achievement. In some situations coaches may have staff supervision and evaluation responsibilities. Some coaches also take on managerial roles, particularly in relation to the collection and interpretation of academic data and the management of the multitude of instructional materials used in today's classrooms.

Any of these activities can be performed by teachers or specialists who are formally designated coaches and who can provide this kind of supportive, collegial role as their job. Some of the key coaching activities can also be performed by someone at a school site who simply has some time available and the knowledge and skills to provide support to her/his colleagues. This person could be a reading specialist, a school counselor, a special educator, or the building principal.

A Framework for Coaching: SAILS

In their how-to manual for reading coaches, Hasbrouck and Denton (2005) suggest that coaching is most successful when it is provided within a systemwide context focused on the success of every student. Their review of research on how to achieve this focus resulted in a model they call "SAILS," which stands for standards, assessments, instruction and intervention, leadership, and schoolwide commitment.

Standards   Providing successful instruction that meets the needs of every student requires a shared understanding of and agreement on what should be taught. Teachers certainly agree with Kroth and Edge (1997) that there is never enough time, money or trained personnel to do the important work of teaching our students. In this age of increasing accountability, it is necessary to focus on the essential skills and strategies that must be taught and learned at each successive grade level. State standards can help provide the road map for planning instruction and evaluating student progress.

Assessments   Professional educators take responsibility for providing the best possible instruction for each and every student. In order to do this, teachers need information and data for making the important and often complex decisions that teaching requires. Four categories of assessments are available to provide different kinds of information to professional educators:

1. Screening assessments provide information about which students are probably on track with their learning and which students may need some extra assistance.

2. Diagnostic assessments provide teachers with information about an individual student's skills strengths and needs.

3. Progress monitoring assessments help teachers determine if their instruction is academically profitable and enhancing students' learning.

4. Outcome assessments help teachers (and administrators and parents) determine if students are making sufficient progress toward reaching the standards for achievement at each grade level.

Instruction and Intervention   The most powerful tool that teachers can use to help students succeed is to design and deliver effective instruction, differentiated to meet the needs of each individual student and targeted to help students learn the skills, strategies, and knowledge to become motivated and competent learners.

Leadership   The job of classroom teachers covers the first three areas of this framework: standards, assessments, and instruction and intervention. Teachers should be aware of the standards and use them to plan instruction, collect and use assessment data for making informed decisions about their students, and design and provide effective instruction to every student. In order for teachers to perform these essential skills at an optimal level, they will need support from leadership. Hasbrouck and Denton (2005) describe leadership as the process of providing vision, guidance, and support to teachers to ensure that (1) effective reading instruction and interventions designed to meet standards are implemented for all students, and (2) instructional decisions are based on continuous assessment data.

Schoolwide Commitment   One of the characteristics of schools in which students consistently meet high standards despite sometimes serious and daunting challenges is adherence to a systemwide "no excuses" perspective that partners administrators, teachers, parents, and staff to help every student achieve success. Challenges? Certainly. Excuses? Never! These schools also encourage and support collaboration across classrooms, special programs, and homes.

Within a comprehensive framework such as SAILS, a coach can work with the building leadership, teachers, and specialists who work directly with students to provide the kind of sustained support that truly brings lasting and important changes to a school.

COACHING DIFFERENTIATED INSTRUCTION

The person who takes on the role of providing support, encouragement, and guidance to his/her colleagues for implementing differentiated instruction needs to have access to a wealth of information as well as the skills and strategies to work collaboratively with other educators and administrators.

What Is the Knowledge Base for Coaching?

A coach helping to make differentiated instruction successful should be familiar with

- common traits of highly successful schools;

- using state-designated instructional standards to set clear goals and benchmarks for the academic success of each student;

- selecting and administering appropriate assessments (for screening, diagnosis, and progress monitoring) and analyzing and using the results for collaboratively planning and monitoring students' learning;

- selecting and evaluating the effectiveness of materials for instruction and intervention; and

- the elements of effective, systematic, explicit, and intensive instruction and intervention.

Resources for this knowledge base are vast and often easily accessible on the Internet. A good place to start is Web sites that focus on reading: the *Florida Center for Reading Research* (www.fcrr.org), *Big Ideas in Beginning Reading* (http://reading.uoregon.edu/), *Reading Rockets* (www.readingrockets.org), *Colorin Colorado* (for English Learners) (www.colorincolorado.org). Some printed materials that should be part of the library of a coach are *The Report of the National Reading Panel*, *Overcoming Dyslexia* (Shaywitz, 2004), *Preventing Reading Difficulties* (Snow, Burns, & Griffith, 2000), and *When Adolescents Can't Read* (Curtis & Longo, 1999). Coaches are often viewed as leaders by their colleagues and should look for opportunities to deepen their own professional knowledge base and leadership skills. Coaches often find support for this role from professional organizations such as the International Reading Association (IRA), the Council for Exceptional Children (CEC), and the Association for Supervision and Curriculum Development (ASCD).

What Is the Skill Base for Coaching?

As was mentioned previously, the role of coach, the person designated to provide sustained and individualized support to teachers who are moving to differentiated instruction, can be assumed by someone who does this as their full-time job or by someone at the school, such as a reading specialist, special educator, school counselor, or principal, as an additional role. The coach should have a deep knowledge of the components of effective instruction, but that alone won't be sufficient for success. Coaching is different from teaching, in large part because it involves working in partnership with a peer. Learning how to form and maintain professional, collaborative relationships with school colleagues is essential for successful coaching.

Goals for Coaching

When coaching is implemented in schools, coaches often work achieving toward four general goals (Hasbrouck & Denton, 2005):

1. Improving students' reading skills and competence

2. Solving the concerns of colleagues related to student success

3. Learning from each other

4. Preventing future concerns

Helping teachers successfully implement the suggestions outlined in this book through collaboration and mutual support will enhance schoolwide efforts toward meeting these goals.

GETTING STARTED

The previous five chapters in this book describe procedures for implementing and managing differentiated instruction in classrooms at all levels. As you read these chapters, we hope you started to get excited about how these methods could be used to provide more effective (and fun!) instruction in your own classrooms. But we also expect that you may have also felt a bit overwhelmed.

The ideas suggested in Chapters 2 through 5 are seldom implemented in the classrooms that most of us are familiar with. While these ideas can sound good, they may seem nearly impossible to implement in a real-world classroom. We can assure you that these ideas have indeed been successfully adopted and implemented by teachers at all grade levels and that they can be used successfully by you!

All successful change in schools happens by following a process that begins with a *vision* of what needs to happen and why, followed by a *plan* that includes sustained guidance and support for implementing the plan. Most teachers would benefit greatly from guidance and support as they begin to create a vision for how they can teach differently and devise a plan for making differentiated instruction occur successfully in their classrooms. However, while coaching enhances the probability of success, teachers can do this without support. Some first steps might include:

- Learning the research base that provides the rationale for differentiated instruction as presented in Chapter 1 and using this knowledge to develop the vision of how this new way of teaching would directly help the teachers and students in your own school.

- Becoming the building "expert" in the processes of classroom and instructional organization described in Chapters 2 through 5. It might include working with a single teacher or a grade-level team of teachers who are eager and ready to undertake this change so that a model could be provided for other teachers to see. Asking for volunteers would be a good place to begin.

- Working with the building principal and colleagues to develop a schoolwide attitude about collaboration and mutual support (for example, understanding why having students copy each other's work can be beneficial and having teachers learn that receiving and providing collaborative support to each other is essential for implementing new information, routines, and procedures).

- Learning how to use data to determine what students need, where to begin instruction, how to analyze error patterns and make instructional decisions, and how to select materials and activities that are academically profitable to enhance student achievement.

- Learning how to evaluate instructional effectiveness, analyze program effectiveness, and determine student achievement in relationship to grade level, district, and state academic requirements.

- Ultimately helping to design a schoolwide implementation plan for helping every colleague make the adjustments so that differentiated instruction is successfully implemented in every classroom and every student is being given the best possible chance to succeed. This involves clearly identifying what needs to change, how it will change, and what timing or pacing is required to create and sustain the change.

The following list includes actions that the person providing coaching support should use to help teachers get started successfully. Some of these areas will need professional development and training *before* the teacher begins to reorganize for differentiated instruction. Other areas will need *ongoing* professional development and support. Teachers appreciate receiving positive constructive feedback and encouragement throughout the change process. The coach can help teachers get started successfully by supporting and participating in decision-making. The coach can help a teacher

- determine *what* to teach—based on an understanding the instruction standards for each grade or content area.

- select, administer, and interpret the results from various assessments for determining students knowledge and needs. Decide how and when to monitor students' progress (observations, work samples, and notes on mailing labels), as well as more formal assessments for screening, diagnosis, and progress monitoring.

- set priorities and sequence instruction based on data and school, state, or national standards.

- develop criteria for how and when to use whole class or small groups for instruction; how and when to use various grouping patterns (homogenous, heterogeneous, or mixed skill levels); and how and when to group within a whole class lesson.

- determine what materials and activities will be academically profitable for increasing student engagement, providing skills-focused instruction, and improving achievement.

PLAN OF ACTION: THE FIRST WEEKS OF SCHOOL

When you are ready to begin, whether you are going to implement these ideas in your own classroom or whether there is a plan to develop a single model classroom or a grade level of model classrooms, there are some important ideas to think about for the first few weeks. It is important to understand that this model of instructional organization is achieved OVER TIME. It is a process of development. Teachers who have been successfully implementing this model of differentiated instruction in their classrooms for years understand that the first week or two of school are used to set the environment for learning by establishing routines and procedures. For this plan to work, students of all ages must be given the time to learn the new skills and establish routines of self-management. Depending on the students' ages, grade level placement, or personalities, this process may take a few weeks. It is ONLY after this time has been devoted to helping the students learn the necessary procedures, behaviors, and routines that skills-focused, formal instruction will begin. First you set the environment for differentiated instruction to occur, then you focus on effective teaching.

Establishing routines and procedures and creating an environment where whole class and small group instruction can occur is time well spent. There will be a lot of learning going on, and this investment in time initially will pay off with huge benefits later. The initial focus is on environmental and behavioral management as part of the bigger responsibility for instruction management. More formal academic instruction will begin after a week or two when students are more familiar with the process needed to differentiate instruction effectively.

The following timeline is a suggestion only. Your own situation may allow you to move through these initial steps more quickly than we are suggesting, or you may need to slow down and take a bit more time. Close observations of your students will help you know when they are ready to move to the next step.

Week One

Your primary focus for week one is behavioral and environmental, not academic. Instruction during week one is aimed at students' independence levels, and activities should review previously learned concepts. The focus during this early stage should be on having students learn the behaviors that will help them succeed once the academic instruction begins. Carefully select workstation or independent activities. Make sure certain routines and procedures are clearly understood and easily completed by your students.

Provide activities that encourage students to talk and cooperate with each other and that require minimal teacher supervision. Instruction during week one is on the independent level so you may provide support for environmental management. Your students will probably need considerable practice to learn to do the routines and procedures successfully. Consider using American Sign Language to cue and manage behaviors without interrupting instructional activities.

These steps will enhance your success during the first week.

- *Create three to four groups of students that can work well together.* These initial groups are not based on academic skill levels as they will be later. For now, these groups are based only on compatibility, so think about grouping students with compliant *behaviors*. Strategically select students to work in groups separating students who cannot work together without teacher supervision. If you have some students who like to take charge, try to distribute them across the groups. Don't worry about getting this "perfect" on the first day. You can make changes to group memberships immediately or as needed. In this model of instructional management, groups are always flexible, so adjustments to group memberships can be made at any time.

- *Physically organize the classroom.* Do this to implement differentiated instruction by setting up workstations, your teaching table, and the worktable.

- *Develop a classroom schedule.* Alternate time periods to include whole class instruction, small group instruction, and activities that may be completed collaboratively or independently at workstations. Discuss the class schedule with your students and stress the importance of working efficiently. Encourage students to complete work at school during each work period so they can avoid completing assignments at home.

- *Prepare workstations for a variety of purposes.* The purposes should be appropriate for your student and classroom needs, for example, homework, language and literacy, vocabulary, spelling and writing, special projects and creative expression, author study, technology, Take Five, math, science, and social studies. Role-play what-if situations that may occur in each workstation. Demonstrate how to resolve potential problems.

- *Develop a job chart and rotation chart.* It should identify clear expectations for community responsibilities or jobs, and visibly help students know what to do, when to do it, and with whom they will participate. Teach students how to read each chart and determine what they should do. Discuss how the rotation chart helps them know what to do, when to do things, and whom they will work with.

- *Assign and teach students' classroom jobs.* Possibilities for jobs include Chart Caller, Counselor or Special Friend, Timekeeper, Trash Monitor, Voice Level Monitor, Mailbox Monitor, Workstation Monitor (Center Checker), Worktable Monitor, Books Monitor, Supply Monitor, Line Leader, Lights Monitor, Recess Assistant, Teaching Assistant, Teacher Assistant, and Correspondent. Role-play to teach expectations about asking for, receiving, and providing assistance.

- *Set up a paper management system.* Use student portfolios or mailboxes, Do/Done folders, and student contracts. Teach students how to use your system through modeling and guided practice.

- *Identify routines and procedures for self-management and collaboration.* Teach your students the routines and procedures for working in small groups, making transitions, and managing their papers and materials. MODEL how they will look. Provide GUIDED PRACTICE with CONSTRUCTIVE FEEDBACK as students walk through the schedule with your help and assistance. When the students seem to have a good understanding of what they should be doing during whole class, small group, and workstation time, provide some INDEPENDENT PRACTICE. Praise their efforts and successes! Be patient and don't expect them—or you!—to get this perfect at the start.

- *Facilitate communication and conflict resolution.* Teach students some basic skills in these areas. This instruction will continue throughout the year as various conflicts and interpersonal challenges arise.

Week Two

Maintain an instructional purpose aimed at your students' independence level and set a perky pace. Continue developing an environment with good routines and procedures. Instruction during your second week should still require minimal teacher assistance, so you are free to monitor, encourage, and assist students as they learn the new structure and routines.

- *PRACTICE, PRACTICE, PRACTICE!* Make adjustments to the grouping memberships as necessary to allow students to be successful in managing their behaviors. You can begin to introduce slightly more challenging activities at the workstations if your students seem to be ready. Continue to praise your students and acknowledge their efforts to cooperate, help each other, and follow the guidelines and procedures.

- Help students who held classroom jobs during week one *train students assigned jobs for week two.*

- Toward the end of week two you can begin *administering assessments* and gathering data that you will use to determine the skill levels of your students and form small groups for skills-focused instruction.

Week Three

When the routines have been established and your classroom is functioning smoothly, it is time to shift your focus to more intense instruction at the teaching table and workstations or worktable. This can happen during week three or sometime during week four. Spending more time initially on creating an environment that allows good instruction to occur ensures you will have time later to catch up on instruction that may have been missed during the first few weeks because you will experience fewer problem behaviors.

- *Continue practicing* the routines and begin collecting and analyzing the assessment data so you can form your instructional groups.

- *Rotate job assignments* so students with responsibilities during week two can train students assigned jobs for week three.

- *Place students into small groups* based on their identified academic and instructional needs, realizing that you may want to create two different sets of grouping arrangements, one for homogeneous or similar skills, and another for heterogeneous, or mixed skill groupings.

- *Plan your whole class, small group, and work station lessons* based on your collected data. Select materials and activities that are academically profitable and can be completed within the time period allowed for students to work on an assignment.

Week Four and the Remainder of the Year

Practiced routines and procedures will help your students become more organized and ready for instruction. Your data collection helps you organize and plan effective instruction. By week four you can begin to provide more intense differentiated instruction in small groups. These steps will enhance your success.

- Determine your instructional purpose and focus, then *explicitly teach to increase student achievement.* Your attention is now on instruction and outcomes for academic performance more than on behavioral and environmental issues.

- *Adjust the grouping arrangements and pacing of instruction* based on observation, work samples, and notes on mailing labels, as well as on more formal progress monitoring assessments. Grouping arrangements change with lesson purpose to be sure that instruction is flexible to students' needs and that every student benefits from your teaching.

- *Each day monitor instructional time and make adjustments* to the classroom schedule as needed to maximize the instructional and learning time for students.

- *Use student contracts* or Do/Done Folders as needed to help keep students focused on their assigned work and to achieve success.

- *Continue rotating the jobs* among your students so all students participate and gain from the leadership opportunities.

- *Continue to acknowledge the successes of your students* in managing their own behaviors and assisting and cooperating with each other's academic learning. If there are some rough spots, MODEL the behaviors you want your students to use, provide opportunities for GUIDED PRACTICE, and then give them the chance to practice INDEPENDENTLY. Encourage students to evaluate and make suggestions for improvement. Actively involve them in the process of teaching and learning at all levels: planning, implementing, participating in group work, and evaluating program effectiveness.

SUMMARY

Coaching can play an important role to help teachers, students, and parents clearly understand the purpose and timing for successfully implementing differentiated instruction. Investing the time to establish a well-managed classroom creates opportunities for powerful instruction to occur throughout the year. With less focus on academics the first couple of weeks, teachers use that time to set routines and procedures for successfully implementing whole class and small group instruction. Once those are in place, teachers can focus their efforts on data-informed practices, flexible grouping, and improved skills-focused instruction, and watch their students succeed like never before.

RESOURCES THAT HELP

Curtis, M. E., & Longo, A. M. (1999). *When Adolescents Can't Read.* Cambridge, MA: Brookline.

Hasbrouck, J., & Denton, C. A. (2005). *The Reading Coach: A How-to Manual for Success.* Longmont, CO: Sopris West.

International Reading Association Literacy Coaching Clearinghouse http://www.literacycoachingonline.org/

National Institute of Child Health and Human Development. (2000). *Report of the National Reading Panel. Teaching children to read: An evidence-based assessment of the scientific research literature on reading and its implications for reading instruction* (NIH Publication No. 00-4769). Washington, DC: U.S. Government Printing Office.

Shaywitz, S. (2003). *Overcoming Dyslexia.* NY: Knopf.

Snow, C. E., Burns, S. M., & Griffin, P. (1998). *Preventing Reading Difficulties in Young Children.* National Research Council. Washington, D.C.: National Academy Press.

Frequently Asked Questions (FAQs)

What do you do when a student...

- is absent or unavailable to complete an assigned job?
  - Assign another student as a substitute or peer partner for the time needed.
- lacks the skills to complete the assigned job independently?
  - Assign more than one student for several jobs and allow students to work together so that all students participate and contribute.
- is uncooperative, refusing to complete a job or make a choice?
  - Call the Counselor to help solve the problem and be prepared to facilitate the discussion as needed, or institute a consequence, such as 15–30 minutes of community service time, which means the student will work and complete another job in the community (classroom or school) at a later time.
- uses inappropriate or disrespectful language when talking to another student or requesting assistance?
  - Discuss the episode privately or call upon the Counselor to offer proper word choices. Institute a consequence if needed for repeated incidences.
- gets off-task or encourages others to get off-task?
  - Call upon the Counselor or check to see if the work assignment and expectations are clear.. Determine if student needs to be reassigned to a different group or needs additional instruction.
- continually copies other students' work and does not work independently?
  - Check to see if the work assignment is too difficult or the student does not understand the expectations for completion. Examine data to determine if the student needs to be assigned to a different group or needs additional instruction.
- assumes the leadership role too seriously and bosses others in group?
  - Talk privately with the student and clearly identify proper decision making, word choices, or behaviors. Role-play to model expectations with individual students or with the whole class.

- is aggressive and endangers the Counselor or other students?

  ○ Deal with potentially dangerous situations or aggressive students yourself. Plan and explain in advance the consequences for inappropriate conduct. Follow through consistently and completely.

- chooses same workstation again and again?

  ○ Eliminate choices and use the Rotation Chart or a Student Contract to direct student to activities.

- refuses to clean up on time during a transition?

  ○ Call the Counselor, Workstation Monitor, or Worktable Monitor to assist the student with cleanup.

- two students cannot work together without teacher assistance?

  ○ Reassign them to different small groups and ensure their groups do not participate in the same place at the same time.

Suggestions for Getting Started

Create Tools for the Management System

1. Assess to collect data about student knowledge and needs.

2. Use data to assign small group memberships and plan instruction.

3. Develop a daily schedule that includes time periods for whole class and small group instruction.

4. Create a job chart, assign responsibilities, and teach expectations.

5. Create a rotation chart, select group names, and teach expectations.

6. Develop workstations and select activities that may be completed within the scheduled work period.

7. Examine curriculum to select activities that are skills focused and aligned to instructional goals.

8. Prepare materials and organize for easy access and use.

9. Teach, review, and reteach as needed.

10. Evaluate system and adjust to student/teacher needs.

Monitor Progress and Evaluate Achievement

1. Create two sets of mailboxes (student portfolios).

   a. A private mailbox that the teacher uses to file assessments and work samples during the year to evaluate achievement

   b. A public mailbox where students deposit and maintain papers in progress, work for the day, notes from or to the teacher, notes to go home, etc.

2. Observe and record comments on mailing labels and file in public mailbox.

3. Save work samples periodically and file in private mailbox.

4. Review all data to maintain skills-focused instruction that is purposeful and academically profitable.

5. Discuss progress by communicating with each student what is needed to increase or maintain achievement.

Finalize the Details

1. Role-play and teach behavioral expectations to establish routines and procedures.

2. Assign activities that require minimal teacher supervision during the first two weeks and focus on routines and procedures for classroom management.

3. Change assignments on the job chart weekly by rotating students' names.

4. Close each day by changing the rotation chart to communicate expectations for next day.

5. Provide skills-focused instruction that benefits every student every day.

Teaching Tips

DEVELOPING INSTRUCTION MANAGEMENT

- What do you do first?
  - Commit to work hard and make a change. Then follow the Suggestions for Getting Started, Appendix B.

- How long does it take to teach this management system to students?
  - Teachers who see the same students every day report their students establish routines and procedures within 3–5 days or sometimes 2–3 weeks. It depends on the age and skill levels of the students and the teacher's skills for communicating clear expectations, consistently teaching and modeling expectations, and providing encouraging feedback for efforts and achievements.

- Is it okay to start now or should one wait until next year?
  - Start immediately to increase teaching time and minimize behavior problems. The opportunities to move, talk, collaborate, and get help encourage positive student behavior.

- Do you need new furniture to create workstations?
  - No, push desks together to create work areas or have students work on the floor using clipboards for a writing surface if table space is limited.

- What activities may be assigned at the workstations?
  - Assign activities that you use now but ensure sufficient instruction has been provided so students can complete the assignment either collaboratively or independently.

- What do I teach in whole class and what do I teach in small groups?
  - Introduce, practice, or review information in whole class, but teach critical skills to mastery in small group.

- How often do I change group memberships?
  - Monitor students' progress and change group memberships to match lesson purpose and compatibility within groups.

- How do you maintain a pace that has time to get everything done?
  - Prepare materials in advance and place in file folders or on a shelf

close to the teaching table. Start the timer and teach purposefully without telling stories and getting off-track.

- How do you get students to make a transition in 5 minutes?
  - Clearly identify expectations for performance. Assign jobs to students. Play music or use a timer to indicate when a transition period begins and ends. Brag on efforts and achievements.

IMPROVING INSTRUCTIONAL EFFECTIVENESS

1. Use data to determine what a student knows and needs, and to monitor progress.

2. Teach differently by introducing, practicing, and reviewing in whole class and teaching skills to mastery in smaller groups.

3. While teaching skills at the Teaching Table, closely observe patterns of error and provide immediate constructive feedback.

4. Use a rotation system so every group meets with the teacher every day.

5. Provide repeated practices during whole and small group lessons using partners to increase engagement.

6. Encourage students to cooperate, collaborate, and provide feedback to each other during practice activities or when you are not available.

7. Teach the language (vocabulary word meanings) in context before any lesson in any academic subject at any grade level so instruction makes sense.

8. Stop frequently, allowing students to summarize by discussing information with a partner or small group. Listen and reteach as needed.

9. Delay assigning any practice activity until sufficient instruction has occurred.

10. Observe to ensure that students have at least 60–70 percent skill mastery BEFORE assigning work to be completed independently as seatwork or homework.

INCREASING ENGAGEMENT AND IMPROVING BEHAVIORAL MANAGEMENT

1. Use routines and procedures to accomplish expectations.

2. Use American Sign Language to positively cue behaviors and communicate without interrupting instruction.

3. Speak in present tense verbs, short sentences, and simple words when giving directions or providing constructive feedback.

4. Use partners to increase student engagement.

5. Use a rotation system that guides students through activities.

6. Compliment compliance, cooperation, and project completions, honoring efforts and achievement.

7. Use a graphic organizer to summarize information after whole or small group discussions where YOU write and students discuss to review information and quickly complete an overview lesson.

8. Implement Take Five by using an area in the classroom with a timer, books, and music of your choice. Students elect to take a 5 minute break and calm down by listening to music and/or reading. This develops self-monitoring and self-regulation skills.

Checklist for Monitoring Instructional Time (C-MIT)

Purpose   Examine use of instructional time

Procedure

- Observe an instructional lesson for 20 minutes.

- Every 15 seconds, place a checkmark in the appropriate column that indicates how the teacher is using instructional time for (B) behavior, (E) environment, or (T) teaching.

- Count to total how many checkmarks are in each column.

- Discuss and determine what changes may be needed to increase more teaching time.

USE TIMER FOR 20 MINUTES TO MONITOR TIME	B BEHAVIOR	E ENVIRONMENT	T TEACHING
Definitions	Teacher is talking and working with student(s), or involved with ANY issue related to behavior.	Teacher is involved with ANY issue related to management of materials or environment.	Teacher is engaged with purposeful lesson and available for immediate feedback.
Place checkmarks in these columns to indicate how instructional time is used.			
Total number of checkmarks			

Teacher Name   Date of Observation

Class Activity Observed

Name of Observer

Comments

Checklist for Monitoring Classroom Environment

Teacher   Date   Observer Name

Observation Period   Time Began _____   Time End_____

Instructional Format   *(Circle number(s) to communicate type of activity observed.)*

CODE	INSTRUCTIONAL FORMATS	DESCRIPTION
1	Whole Class	Teacher directs activity with whole class
2	Small Group - Teaching Table	Teacher directs activity with small group
3	Small Group - Worktable	Teacher monitors & provides minimal assistance as students begin or complete homework assignments
4	Workstations	Students work collaboratively or independently in workstations

Classroom Environment: Observe classroom and mark "NA" if not applicable.

Yes	No	Tools or Areas	Description
		Mailboxes	Hanging file folders used as portfolios
		Job Chart	Chart used to delegate classroom duties
		Daily Schedule	Copy of schedule posted to identify routines for activities
		Rotation Chart	Chart that guides students to activities
		Teaching Table	Area or space for small group work that is teacher-directed
		Worktable	Area or space for homework completed in small group work
		Workstations, desks, tables	Area(s) for collaborative small group or independent work
		Reading Materials shared by teacher	Easel or table with materials displayed for reading (books, literature, poetry)
		Language & Literacy Center	Center that includes books, writing, & art materials to integrate reading & writing
		Creative Development Center	Center that contains materials that enhance fine & large motor development (puzzles, books, creative writing & art materials)
		Area for displaying student work	Area where students' work is displayed
		Math & Science Center	Discovery center for math & science experiences
		Technology Center	Computers with software to support skills instruction

Teacher/Classroom Observation Report (T-COR)

Teacher Name _____   Class/Grade _____

Date of Observation _____   Time of Observation _____

Observer Name _____   Activity Observed _____

COMMENTS/RECOMMENDATIONS	OBSERVATIONS
Instruction	___Teacher appears prepared & organized. ___Materials appear ready & accessible. ___Purpose of instruction is stated & clear. ___Teacher links prior instruction to new. ___Skills taught appear appropriate. ___Pacing is appropriate. ___Opportunities for students to participate. ___Teacher modifies instruction as needed. ___Teacher questions to check understanding. ___Teacher summarizes to review & close.
Environment	___Classroom appears orderly & clean. ___Expectations appear to be clear. ___Management system appears effective. ___Students' work is displayed. ___Materials are stored appropriately. ___Environment feels managed & in control. ___Atmosphere is friendly & caring. ___Students appear engaged & learning.
Management	___Order is maintained. ___Student behaviors are positive & interactive. ___Noise level is appropriate. ___Behaviors are appropriate. ___Positive rapport shared in classroom. ___Personal needs of students addressed. ___Students receiving assistance as needed. ___Students encouraged to make choices. ___Students encouraged to act responsibly. ___Teacher responding respectfully. ___Teacher honoring students in classroom. ___Time used efficiently & effectively.
Comments/Suggestions	

Administrator or supervisors, parents, & visitors are encouraged to provide positively stated comments that help improve instructional & behavioral skills. Add comments & suggestions on back if needed.

Person completing this form _____ Title _____

Name of teacher observed _____ Grade _____

Age of students in group _____ Number of students observed _____

Time/length of observation _____ Observed teaching ___ yes ___ no

---

Add positively stated comments that reflect your observations or experiences today. If there was no opportunity to observe, note in your comments as "Not Observed."

---

1. Summarize your observations about the teacher's attitude and role as a classroom manager.

2. Summarize your observations of the classroom environment and students' interactions.

3. Summarize students' reactions to instructional activities (i.e., students appear to know what is expected, are allowed to ask questions or seek help, assistance is provided by peer or teacher).

4. State strengths & positive attributes for time management (i.e., instructional pace was appropriate; students actively involved with learning experiences that were meaningful and purposeful).

5. Suggest what is needed for professional development to improve classroom management or instruction.

ADDITIONAL COMMENTS

Plan of Assistance for Personal and Professional Development

S = *Strong*   *A* = *Acceptable*   *NI* = *Needs Improvement*   *NA* = *No Opportunity to Observe*

1. Works cooperatively with supervisors, teachers, students, and other staff.   1. ____

2. Completes assigned tasks/duties/assignments promptly, responsibly, and with acceptable quality.   2. ____

3. Accepts constructive feedback and uses the information for professional growth and improvement.   3. ____

4. Exhibits flexibility in dealing with students, families, and staff.   4. ____

5. Uses appropriate and professional written and spoken language.   5. ____

6. Promptly uses appropriate channels for solving interpersonal or professional conflicts or concerns.   6. ____

7. Maintains appropriate professional appearance and demeanor.   7. ____

8. Maintains and respects confidentiality and rights to privacy of students, families, and colleagues in all professional interactions.   8. ____

9. Demonstrates sensitivity to and acceptance of the diverse cultural backgrounds of students and families.   9. ____

10. Demonstrates instructional effectiveness in classroom teaching as evaluated by supervisor(s).   10. ____

Employee Name/Signature: _____   Date: _____

Person Completing Form Name/Signature: _____   Date: _____

Expectations and Support for Employee

Goals to be met: As measured by:

Assistance to be provided:

Person providing support:

1.

2.

3.

4.

5.

Agreement for Professional Development Coaching and Support
Development and efforts toward attaining goals are expected to begin on this
date: _____ with periodic reviews by _____ (name of
person responsible for providing support).
Reviews and consultation will occur on this schedule:

_____

_____

Supervisor/Date   **Employee Signature/Date**

_____

Mentor or Coach/Date

Graphic Organizer for Daily or Weekly Overviews

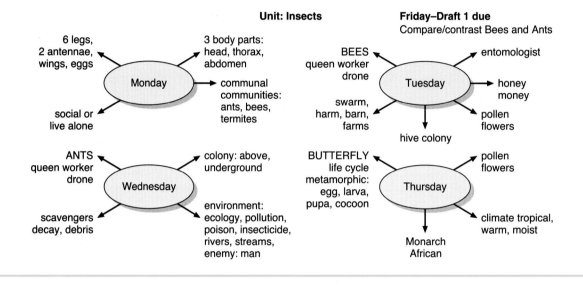

This graphic organizer was completed by a teacher for a thematic lesson on insects. It was developed from instruction for one week. Teachers use a graphic organizer to introduce, practice, and help students learn vocabulary words and key concepts related to each week's instruction.

Use instructional time efficiently and effectively.
Teachers present the daily lesson, then complete part of the graphic organizer. The four bubbles on this illustration represent daily instruction for Monday through Thursday, with a written assignment due on Friday. Notice the written assignment for Friday posted at the top right corner. Some teachers prefer to add a fifth bubble in the middle of the page and use it on Friday to summarize the main idea or big themes of the week.

Increase student engagement and keep a perky pace of instruction.
Each daily bubble represents the key vocabulary words or concepts from a 10–15 minute overview lesson to the whole class. Students listen and observe while their teacher models and presents a lesson. Frequently the teacher asks students to turn

to a person next to them, to an assigned partner, or to members in a small group and paraphrase or discuss the teacher's instruction, linking old and new information. The teacher models expectations for participation by subvocalizing the correct response:

TEACHER: *"Tell the person next to you that insects have three body parts."*

Students turn and prepare to talk.

TEACHER: *"Insects have three body parts."*

Students repeat along with teacher.

TEACHER: *"Correct. Insects have three body parts."*

As the week progresses, teacher support and lecture time may decrease to allow longer periods for small group discussion.

Chunk information and teach more efficiently and effectively.

The graphic organizer helps teachers present and review information consistently. It provides a visual for correct spellings of key words or phrases that helps students recall information. Teachers use the organizer during morning overviews and at the end of class periods to provide repeated practice opportunities. The graphic organizer becomes a one-page "cheat sheet" that allows easier access to newly presented information.

Model and teach using a visual so students look, listen, and learn, not write.

Teachers develop the organizer by writing on a transparency using an overhead projector or by drawing it on chart paper during the lesson or immediately following it. Students listen, look, and verbalize what they are learning. They do not write or copy anything while the teacher is completing the graphic organizer. Expecting students to print along with the teacher may not permit keeping a perky pace of instruction. Having students print or copy the words from the chart is NOT the main objective anyway. The teacher develops the organizer to demonstrate a process or strategy for synthesizing a lot of information and organizing it to facilitate comprehension. The graphic organizer is a teacher-created study tool for students.

Use partnering to increase practice opportunities.

After completing a bubble on the graphic organizer each day, teachers divide their students into partners or in small groups (2 students are assigned as partners or 4–8 students may be assigned to a small group). The partnerships or groups include mixed skill levels to enhance discussions and ensure corrective feedback is available.

Teachers ask students to repeat information to their partners or group members:

TEACHER: *"Listen first, then say this word with me, /en//to//mo/lo//gist/. Practice with me, /en//to//mo//lo//gist/."*

TEACHER: *"Turn to your partner and say, /en//to//mo//lo//gist/. Do it now please."*

Students turn to partner and sound out the word, /en//to//mo//lo//gist/.

TEACHER: *"Clap and say the syllables that you hear, /en//to//mo//lo//gist/."*

Students follow the teacher's model and repeat it to a partner or small group.

TEACHER: *"I hear five parts in that word, /en//to//mo//lo//gist/. Clap it with me and listen for five parts (or syllables)."*

Students clap and say the sound parts of the word with the teacher.

Students may be asked to repeat words or provide short definitions of a word or to use a word in an oral sentence. They may discuss concepts or respond to teacher questions with their partners or in the small groups. Whatever the expectation is by the teacher, the teacher models and provides support until sufficient instruction has been provided that students can respond independently with success. Students within the group are encouraged to provide immediate assistance and positive corrective feedback. The partners and small groups function as collaborative, cooperative study groups.

Pace instruction and review content each day of the week.

Instruction begins on Monday with the teacher introducing the lesson to the whole class (approximately 10–15 minutes). The teacher closes the lesson by printing words or phrases on a graphic organizer to summarize information taught that day. Some teachers draw icons or small pictures to support word meaning as needed.

All students observe and add verbal input as the teacher prints essential information on the graphic organizer. Some teachers have students engage in dialogue to practice with a partner or in a small group after each addition to the graphic organizer. Stopping frequently and allowing students to practice appears to help younger children or more at-risk students.

Assign partners within small groups.

Partners and small student groups are used for guided practice. Stronger skilled students lead the discussions on newly presented information. Students with average performance skills or those that need a little more assistance lead discussions of previously taught content. Students requiring more support are allowed more instruction and modeling before they are asked to respond in the face of their peers. All students participate without being placed at risk for not knowing information or being unable to make a contribution.

Teachers assign a number to each student within each partnership or group, that is, 1, 2 or 1. 2. 3. 4., etc. The numbers are used by teachers to direct student responses during guided practice activities. Students assigned as number 1 should have higher skill levels or mastery. Students assigned as number 2 should be on grade level with average skills. Students assigned as number 3 are working below grade level, etc.

NOTE: Vary the way numbers are assigned each week, that is, the following week the teacher may assign number 1 to lesser skilled students, number 2 to the higher skilled students, and number 3 to average skilled students. The purpose for using numbers is NOT to identify skill levels. The numbers are used by the teacher to direct participation in activities. This ensures that all students participate and no student is embarrassed or asked to do something before sufficient instruction and modeling have been provided.

An example of the dialogue for using partnering in this format would be:

TEACHER: *Partner 1 tell partners 2, 3, 4 that an insect has six legs and three body parts. Do it now please."* (Teacher subvocalizes the response for support if needed by saying, "Insects have six legs and three body parts.")

Partner 1 turns and says to Partners 2, 3, 4, "Insects have six legs and three body parts."

TEACHER: *Partners 2, 3, 4. . . Did Partner 1 say that insects have six legs and three body parts? If so, show me a thumbs up."*

Partners 2, 3, 4 signal to the teacher with a thumbs up.

TEACHER: *Partner 2, tell partners 1, 3, 4, how many legs that insects have. . . . six . . . they have six legs. Do it now please."*

Partner 2 tells partners: "Insects have six legs."

TEACHER: *Partners 1, 3, 4...show me a thumbs up if Partner 2 said that insects have six legs."*

TEACHER: *Partner 3 . . . tell partners 1, 2, 4 how many body parts that insects have . . . . three . . . three body parts. Do that now please."*

Partner 3 turns to other partners and repeats, "Insects have three body parts".

TEACHER: *Partners 1, 2, 4...show me a thumbs up if Partner 3 said that insects have three body parts."*

Students signal with a thumbs up to indicate approval or agreement.

Teacher now turns to Partner 4, assuming these students need additional support...which they have received by the former modeling, guided practice, and feedback.

TEACHER: *Partner 4, tell your partners how many legs and body parts can we find on an insect. . . . six legs, three body parts. Say it with me. . . .six legs, three body parts."*

Partner 4 repeats with teacher: six legs, three body parts.

TEACHER: *Partner 4, turn and tell your partners how many legs and body parts can be found on an insect. . . .six legs, three body parts. Do it now please."*

Partner 4 turns and follows instruction from the teacher, telling partners that insects have six legs and three body parts.
0
This example illustrates the sequence of instruction for an introductory explicit teach. It feels redundant, but it illustrates some key points. Students need more modeling and support initially. They need more repeated practice with each of them participating. The instruction needs to be fast-paced and include opportunities for students to hear, see, say, and do something to stay engaged.

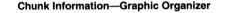

Chunk Information—Graphic Organizer

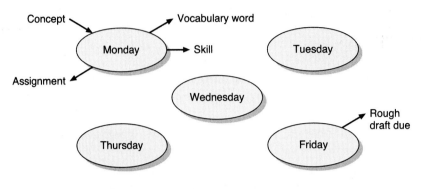

Notice that Partners 3 and 4, assumed in this example to be students with weaker skills, have the privilege of more modeling before they are asked to participate in the face of their peers. Also, know that all students are encouraged to provide immediate positive corrective feedback at all times during the practice lessons.

Link old and new instruction.
Each day, the previously taught material (introduced first on Monday) is reviewed quickly by the teacher to link old and new information. The same lesson format is used during each daily overview, i.e., a 10–15 minute lecture followed by student partners or small groups discussing the information: The teacher walks around the room as students discuss information to determine if more instruction on a particular concept is needed. Using modeling and lecture formats followed by collaborative discussions, student participation increases and multiple repeated practice opportunities are created for all students.

Extend the lesson.
Teachers use the graphic organizer as a reference guide for other activities. They may ask questions and expect students to respond to them, that is, "Name three characteristics of insects." The graphic organizer summarizes information and makes it easily accessible. Some teachers allow students to use the graphic organizer for instructional support during written assignments, that is, "Create a Venn diagram that illustrates how bees and ants are the same or alike." Many teachers allow students to use the graphic organizer to respond to questions on assessments that involve higher order thinking and application.

Increase instructional effectiveness.
The graphic organizer illustrated at the beginning of this document correlates to a thematic unit on insects. Other information could be added if there were more space, but overload is not recommended. Vocabulary words and concepts essential for comprehension are listed on the graphic organizer. Follow this weekly format to present instruction:

Monday Teacher presents lesson, then Partner 1, or a highly skilled partner, leads a 2 minute discussion for the small group of students and basically summarizes information that was just presented. Teacher walks around providing positive corrective feedback as needed.

Tuesday The teacher reviews the information on the graphic organizer for Monday to link previously taught information to new information. After completing a 10 minute whole class lesson, the teacher adds more information to the graphic organizer using the bubble marked Tuesday. Then Partner 2, an average skilled student, summarizes the content from Monday and Partner 1, a highly skilled student, summarizes the content from Tuesday.

Wednesday The teacher reviews briefly the information from Monday and Tuesday to link old and new content, then he/she presents the lesson on Wednesday and completes the bubble marked, Wednesday. Partner 3, a lesser skilled student, reviews information from Monday (because she/he has had numerous practices with the content on Monday and Tuesday). Partner 2 reviews information from Tuesday, and Partner 1 reviews information from Wednesday.

Thursday The teacher briefly reviews information from Monday to Wednesday, then presents the lesson for Thursday. She/he adds information on the graphic organizer using the bubble marked Thursday. Students discuss within small groups. Partner 3 leads discussion for Monday and Tuesday, Partner 2 leads the review for Wednesday, and Partner 1 reviews the information for Thursday. The teacher leads a discussion or encourages students to work in small groups and compare and contrast the information about bees and ants because a rough draft is due the following day for that assignment.

Friday Students may work in small groups and collectively draft a paper comparing and contrasting Bees and Ants, or students may work alone using the graphic organizer for information, vocabulary, and correct spelling.

Create a weekly summary sheet, or "cheat sheet."
The teacher duplicates the graphic organizer on Friday and provides a copy for each student. It can be used to review or as a reference guide for written assignments. Some teachers attach student work samples to the graphic organizer and send the packet home on Fridays. Often teachers begin the next week's instruction using the completed graphic organizer on Monday to link last week's information to the current week's vocabulary and concepts.

REFERENCES

Abadzi, H. (1985). Ability grouping effects on academic achievement and self-esteem: Who performs in the long run as expected. *Journal of Educational Research, 79*(1), 36–40.

Adams, M. J. (1990). *Beginning to Read: Thinking and Learning About Print.* Cambridge, MA: MIT Press.

Annenberg Institute for School Reform. (2004). *Instructional Coaching: Professional Development Strategies that Improve Instruction.* Providence, RI: Brown University, Author.

Barr, R., & Dreeben, R. (1991). Grouping students for reading instruction. In R. Barr, M. L. Kamil, P. B. Mosenthal, & P. D. Pearson (Eds.), *Handbook of reading research:* Vol. II, (pp. 885–910). New York: Longman.

Bean, R. M., Swan, A. L., & Knaub, R. (2003). Reading specialists in schools with exemplary reading programs: Functional, versatile, and prepared. *The Reading Teacher, 56*(5), 446–455.

Bloom, B. S. (1984). The 2-sigma problem: The search for method of group instruction as effective as one-to-one tutoring. *Educational Researcher, 13,* 4–16.

Calfee, R., & Brown, R. (1979). Grouping students for instruction. In D. L. Duke (Ed.), *Classroom management: Seventy-eighth yearbook of the National Society for the Study of Education* (pp. 144–182). Chicago: University of Chicago Press.

Carnine, D. (1997). Bridging the research-to-practice gap. *Exceptional Children, 63*(4), 513–521.

Carnine, D. (1999). Perspective: Campaigns for moving research to practice. *Remedial and Special Education, 20*(1), 2–9.

Carnine, D. W., Silbert, J., & Kame'enui, E. J. (1997). *Direct Instruction Reading,* 3rd ed. Upper Saddle River, NJ: Prentice Hall.

Carnine, D., Silbert, J., Kame'enui, E., and Tarver, S. (2004). *Direct Reading Instruction,* 4th ed. Upper Saddle River, NJ: Prentice Hall.

Come, B., & Fredericks, A.D. (1995). Family literacy in urban schools: Meeting the needs of at risk children. *The Reading Teacher, 48(7),* 566–571.

Elbaum, B., Moody, S., & Schumm, J. S. (1999). Mixed-ability grouping for reading: What students think? *Learning Disabilities Research and Practice, 14,* 61–66.

Elbaum, B., Vaughn, S., Hughes, M., & Moody, S. (1998). Grouping practices and reading outcomes for students with disabilities. *Exceptional Children, 65*(3), 399–425.

Elbaum, B., Vaughn, S., Hughes, M., Moody, S. W., & Schumm, J. S. (2000a). How effective are one-to-one tutoring programs in reading for elementary students at risk for reading failure? *Journal of Educational Psychology, 92*(4), 605–619.

Elbaum, B., Vaughn, S., Hughes, M., Moody, S. W., & Schumm, J.S. (2000b). How reading outcomes of students with disabilities are related to instructional grouping formats. A meta-analysis review. In R. Gersten, E. Schiller, & S. Vaughn (Eds.), *Contemporary Special Education Research* (pp. 105–135). Mahwah, NJ: Erlbaum.

Elbaum, B., Vaughn, S., Hughes, M., Moody, S. W., & Schumm, J. S. (2000c). A meta-analytic review of the effect of instructional grouping format on the reading outcomes of students with disabilities. In R. Gersten, E. Schiller, J. S. Schumm, & S. Vaughn (Eds.), *Issues and research in special education* (pp. 105–135). Hillsdale, NJ: Erlbaum.

Farrell, L., Hancock, C., & Smartt, S. (2002). *DIBELS: A Practical Guide for Teachers and Administrators.* Longmont, CO: Sopris West Educational Publishers.

Flood, J., Lapp, D., Flood, S., & Nagel, G. (1992). Am I allowed to group? Using flexible patterns for effective instruction. *The Reading Teacher, 45*(8), 608–616.

Foorman, B. R., & Torgesen, J. (2001). Critical elements of classroom and small group instruction promote reading success in all children. *Learning Disabilities Research and Practice, 16*(4), 203–212.

Fountas, I., & Pinnell, G. (1996). *Guided Reading: Good First Teaching for All Children.* Portsmouth, NH: Heinemann.

Fuchs, D., Fuchs, L. S., & Compton, D. (2004). Identifying reading disability by responsiveness-to-instruction: Specifying measures and criteria. *Learning Disability Quarterly, 27,* 216–227.

Fuchs, D., Fuchs, L. S., Mathes, P. G., & Simmons, D. C. (1997). Peer-assisted learning strategies: Making classrooms more responsive to diversity. *American Education Research Journal, 34*(1), 174–206.

Gersten, R., Vaughn, S., Deshler, D., & Schiller, E. (1997). What we know about using research findings: Implications for improving special education practice. *Journal of Learning Disabilities,* 30(5), 466–476.

Goldenberg, C. (1993). Instructional conversations: Promoting comprehension through discussion. *The Reading Teacher, 46*(4), 316–326.

Good, T. L., & Stipek, D. J. (1983). Individual differences in the classroom: A psychological perspective. In G. D. Fenstermacher & J. I. Goodlad (Eds.), *Individual differences and the common curriculum, Eighty-second yearbook of the National Society for the Study of Education* (pp. 9–43). Chicago: University of Chicago Press.

Hall, S. (2004). *I've "DIBEL'd"—Now What? Determining Intervention With DIBELS.* Longmont, CO: Sopris West Educational Publishers.

Hall, T. (2002). *Differentiated Instruction.* Wakefield, MA: National Center on Accessing the General Curriculum. Retrieved 2006 from www.cast.org/publicatins/ncac/ncac_diffinstruc.html

Hart, B., & Risley, T. (1995). *Meaningful Differences in the Everyday Experience of Young American Children.* York, PA: Brookes.

Hiebert, E. H. (1983). An examination of ability grouping for reading instruction. *Reading Research Quarterly, 4*(2), 213–255.

Johnson, D. W., & Johnson, R. T. (1975). *Learning Together and Alone: Cooperation, Competition, and Individualization.* Englewood Cliffs, NJ: Prentice Hall.

Kosanovich, M., Ladinsky, K., Nelson, L., & Torgesen, J. (2006). *Differentiated Reading Instruction: Small Group Alternative Lesson Structures for All Students,* Guidance Document for Florida Reading First Schools, Just Read, Florida! Florida Center for Reading Research (FCRR).

Kroth, R. L., & Edge, D. (1997). *Strategies for Communicating With Parents and Families of Exceptional Children,* 4th ed. Denver: Love Publishing.

Kulik, J. A. (1992). *An Analysis of the Research on Ability Grouping: Historical and Contemporary Perspective* (RBDM 9204). Storrs, CT: University of Connecticut, National Research Center on the Gifted and Talented.

Labo, L. D., & Teele, W. H. (1990). Cross-age reading: A strategy for helping poor readers. *The Reading Teacher, 43*(6), 362–369.

Lou, Y., Abrami, P. D., Spence, J. C., Poulsen, C., Chambers, B., & d'Apollonia, S. (1996). Within-class grouping: A meta-analysis. *Review of Educational Research, 66*(4), 423–458.

Lyon, G. R. (1995). Research initiatives in learning disabilities: Contributions from scientists supported by the National Institute of Child Health and Human Development. *Journal of Child Neurology, 10,* S121–S126.

Maheady, L. (1997). Preparing teachers for instructing multiple ability groups. *Teacher Education and Special Education, 20,* 322–339.

Marzano, R. (2003). *Classroom Management That Works: Research-Based Strategies for Every Teacher.* Alexandria, VA: Association for Supervision and Curriculum Development.

Mathes, P., Denton, C., Fletcher, J., Anthony, J., Francis, D., & Schatschneider, C. (2005). The effects of theoretically different instruction and student characteristics on the skills of struggling readers. *Reading Research Quarterly, 40*(2), 148–182.

Mathes, P. G., & Fuchs, L. S. (1994). The efficacy of peer tutoring in reading for students with mild disabilities: A best-evidence synthesis. *School Psychology Review, 23*(1), 59–80.

McIntosh, R., Vaughn, S., Schumm, J., Haager, D., & Lee, O. (1993). Observations of students with learning disabilities in general educational classrooms. *Exceptional Children, 60(3),* 249–261.

Moody, S. Vaughn, S., & Schumm, J. (1997). Instructional grouping for reading. *Remedial and Special Education, 18*(6), 347–356.

National Assessment of Educational Progress. (1995). NAEP 1994 reading. A first look: Findings from the national assessment of educational progress, Rev. ed. Washington, DC: U.S. Government Printing Office.

National Institute for Literacy. (2002). *Put Reading First: The Research Building Blocks for Teaching Children to Read.* Jessup, MD: Author.

National Literacy Panel. (2006). *Developing Literacy in Second-Language Learners; Report of the National Literacy Panel on Language-Minority Children and Youth.* D. August & T. Shanahan (Eds.). Center for Applied Linguistics and SRI International by the U.S. Department of Education's Institute of Education Science and the Office of English Language Acquisition.

National Reading Panel. (2000). *Teaching children to read: An evidence-based assessment of the scientific research literature on reading and its implications for reading instruction.* Reports of the subgroup. Bethesda: MD: National Institute of Child Health and Human Development, National Institutes of Health.

National Research Council. (1999). *Starting Out Right: A Guide to Promoting Children's Reading Success.* S. Burns, P. Griffin, & C. Snow (Eds.), Washington DC: National Academy Press.

Rosenholtz, S. J., & Wilson, B. (1980). The effect of classroom structure on shared perceptions of ability. *American Education Research Journal, 17,* 75–82.

Schumm, J. S., Moody, S. W., & Vaughn, S. R. (2000). Grouping for reading instruction: Does one size fit all? *Journal of Learning Disabilities, 33*(5), 477–488.

Slavin, R. E. (1983). Ability grouping and student achievement in elementary schools: A best-evidence synthesis. *Review of Educational Research, 57,* 347–336.

Slavin, R. E. (1987). Ability grouping in elementary schools: Do we really know nothing until we know everything? *Review of Educational Research, 57,* 347–350.

Slavin, R. E. (1988). Synthesis of research on grouping in elementary and secondary schools. *Education Leadership, 46*(1), 67–75.

Thurlow, M. L., Ysseldyke, J. E., Wotruba, J. W., & Algozzine, B. (1993). Instruction in special education classrooms under varying student-teacher ratios. *The Elementary School Journal, 93*(3), 305–320.

Tileston, D. W. (2000). *10 Best Teaching Practices: How Brain Research, Learning Styles, and Standards Define Teaching Competencies.* Thousand Oaks, CA: Corwin Press.

Tilly, W. D. (2003). *How many tiers are needed for successful prevention and early intervention?* Heartland Area Education Agency's Evolution from Four to Three Tiers. Paper presented at the National Research Center on Learning Disabilities Responsiveness-to-Intervention Symposium, Kansas City, MO.

Tomlinson, C. A. (1995). *How to Differentiate Instruction in Mixed-Ability Classrooms.* Arlington, VA: American Association of School Administrators.

Tomlinson, C. A. (1999). *Leadership for Differentiated Classrooms.* Arlington, VA: American Association of School Administrators. [Excerpt from C. A. Tomlinson (1995), *How to Differentiate Instruction in Mixed-Ability Classrooms].*

Tomlinson, C. S., & Eidson, C. C. (2003). *Differentiation in Practice: A Resource Guide for Differentiating Curriculum Grades K–5.* Arlington, VA: American Association of School Administrators.

Tyner, B., & Green, S. (2004). *Small-Group Reading Instruction: A Differentiated Teaching Model for Beginning and Struggling Readers, Grades 3–8.* Newark, DE: International Reading Association.

Vaughn, S. (2003). *How many tiers are needed for response to intervention to achieve acceptable prevention outcomes?* Paper presented at the National Research Center on Learning Disabilities Responsiveness-to-Intervention Symposium, Kansas City, MO.

Vaughn, S., & Chard, D. (1999). *Determining the effectiveness of three grouping formats on the reading progress of struggling readers*. Report submitted to the Texas Education Agency.

Vaughn, S., Hughes, M., Moody, S., & Elbaum, B. (1998). Instructional grouping for reading for students with learning disabilities: Implications for practice. *Intervention in School and Clinic, 36*(3), 131–137.

Vaughn, S., Hughes, M., Moody, S., & Elbaum, B. (2001). Grouping students who struggle with reading. Excerpt from Instructional Grouping for Students with LD: Implications for Practice. *Intervention in School and Clinic, 36*(3), 131–137.

Vaughn, S.R., & Linan-Thompson, S. (2004). *Research-Based Methods of Reading Instruction for Grades K-3*. Alexandria, VA: Association for Supervision and Curriculum Development.

Vaughn, S., Linan-Thompson, S., Kouzekanani, K., Bryant, D. P., Dickson, S., & Blozis, S. A. (2003). Reading instruction grouping for students with reading difficulties. *Remedial and Special Education, 24*(5), 301–315.

Vaughn, S. R., Moody, S. W., & Schumm, J. S. (1998). Broken promises: Reading instruction in the resource room. *Exceptional Children, 64*(2), 211–226.

United States Department of Education (2002). *To assure the free appropriate public education of all children with disabilities*. Twenty-fourth Annual Report to Congress on the Implementation of the Individuals with Disabilities Education Act. Washington, DC: Author.

INDEX